Journey Through the Night

Jakob Littner's
Holocaust Memoir

Kurt Nathan Grübler
With a Foreword by
Reinhard Zachau

CONTINUUM
NEW YORK   LONDON

2000

The Continuum International Publishing Group Inc
370 Lexington Avenue, New York, NY 10017

The Continuum International Publishing Group Ltd
Wellington House, 125 Strand, London WC2R 0BB

Printed in the United States of America

Library of Congress Cataloging-in-Publication Data

Littner, Jakob, 1883-1950.
    [Aufzeichnungen aus einem Erdloch. English]
    Journey through the night : Jakob Littner's Holocaust memoir /
[translated and edited by] Kurt Nathan Grübler ; with a foreword
by Reinhard Zachau.
        p. cm.
    "With additional family and historical material"—Publisher's
information.
    ISBN 0-8264-1197-5
    1. Littner, Jakob, 1883-1950.   2. Jews--Ukraine--Biography.
3. Holocaust, Jewish (1939-1945)—Ukraine—Zbarazh—Personal
narratives.   4. Jews—Germany—Munich—Biography.
I. Grübler, Kurt Nathan, 1925-   II. Title.

DS135.U43 L585 2000
940.53'18'092—dc21
[B]
                                                    00-023191

An unseren lieben
Davis und seinen lieben
zur freundlichen
Erinnerung
Janina und Jenö Littner
New York, Corona den 31/XII 1949

To our dear
Davis and his dear ones
for a friendly remembrance
Janina and Jenö Littner
New York, Corona December 31, 1949
Jenö Littner

Contents

Foreword
The Story of a Book

When Wolfgang Koeppen's *Jakob Littners Aufzeichnungen aus einem Erdloch* (Jakob Littner's notes from a hole in the ground [Frankfurt: Jüdischer Verlag im Suhrkamp Verlag]) was published in 1992 it caused a sensation. The public had long been waiting for a new novel from Koeppen after his successful novels *Tauben im Gras* (1951), *Das Treibhaus* (1953), and *Tod in Rom* (1954). Finally another masterpiece of the eighty-five-year old author appeared, which, according to Ian Buruma, is the only novel written by a gentile German writer that deals directly with the Holocaust, that is, "not metaphorically, or in passing, but . . . actually describes, in fictional terms, the destruction of the Jews." Littner's survival of SS raids within a small Ukrainian town was narrated as a work of fiction, which included the selfless help of a gentile German friend, written in an impressive literary style. The eloquent description of events left many reviewers awestruck, but it was difficult for them to believe that Koeppen invented all of this.

When critics started to research the background of this book, they soon learned that it had previously been published as Jakob Littner's book *Aufzeichungen aus einem Erdloch* (Munich: Kluger, 1948) without any mention of Koeppen. The only changes between the 1948 and 1992 edition consisted of the addition of Koeppen's name as author, the subtitle *Roman* (novel), which he added at the request of his publisher, Suhrkamp, and a foreword by Koeppen. In his foreword, Koeppen referred to notes he had received from a genuine Jakob Littner. Koeppen writes that he had used these notes in 1948 for writing a book at the request of his publisher:

> The Jew told his new publisher that God had held his hand over him. The publisher listened and recorded places and dates. The escaped Jew was looking for a writer. The publisher reported the incredible events to me. I had dreamed of them. The publisher asked me: "Do you want to write it down?" (*Aufzeichnungen aus einem Erdloch*, 6)

Koeppen's critics were puzzled by his concealment of the origin of this manuscript: some people assumed that he fabricated most of its content; others wished
to find out more. Most critics inquired about the questionable ethics of rewriting
an original Holocaust text. Daniel Ganzfried's words written about Binjamin
Wilkomirski's spurious Holocaust book *Fragments* that "when it comes to Auschwitz,
it is essential to tell the truth" could also be applied to Koeppen's book (Elena
Lappin, *The Man with Two Heads* [London: Granta, 1998], 23). How many changes
did Koeppen make in the original text, and how much of his own imagination went
into this version? Koeppen's right as a non-Jewish German to evaluate the events in
his supposedly fictional account was severely criticized: "I hate no one. I do not hate
the guilty ones either. While suffering from their persecutions, I do not wish to be
their judge. God alone may judge the inhumane and he shall judge with mercy,
whereby every human act of mercy would be pretentious" (Koeppen, 149). No
German writer had the right in 1948 to place these words into the mouth of a ficti-
tious Jewish character. However, these questions remained academic since no original text existed. The circumstances remained puzzling since Koeppen died in 1995,
while having made only cursory remarks about his book.

In 1992, the critic Franz Josef Görtz uncovered the fact that Littner had resided
in Munich from 1911 to 1939 and then again from 1945 to July 1947, when he emi-
grated to the United States. He also owned a stamp business at Munich's Karlsplatz
and left Munich on March 1, 1939, in the direction of Prague. Görtz also examined
photos dating from July 1935 in Munich's municipal archive and saw a picture of
Jakob Littner's stamp business. From Paul Conrid, the "Nestor of Munich's stamp col-
lectors," Görtz found out that the woman Koeppen referred to as Christa in his book
was really Christine Hintermaier, who was Littner's friend and business partner. She
continued to manage his business after 1940. Görtz also discovered that Jakob
Littner had lived as a subtenant from August 1 to September 7, 1945, at Christine
Hintermaier's place with his Polish wife, Janina, and a child. From September 1945
until the end of June 1947, Littner had lived in Munich at Bauerstraße, and then he
had gone from Munich to New York, where one of his daughters from his first mar-
riage lived.

With this information I tried to find out from American immigration documents
whether Jakob Littner had really arrived in the United States in July 1947. I found the
confirmation through the "National Archives Ship Passenger Arrival Records" in the

National Archives in Washington, D.C., according to which Jakob Littner, "age 54, citizen of Hungary, accompanied by Janina, 47" had landed in New York on July 17, 1947. His address was given as 522 5th Avenue, New York, N.Y. Here I had the confirmation that Koeppen's book was based on a real person. But it was not clear if Littner had compiled the report himself or whether Koeppen's book was based on "notes on two or three scraps of paper," as his publisher, Suhrkamp, claimed.

Neither an inquiry at Littner's address nor further inquiries at the Leo Baeck Institute archive, the Joint Distribution Committee, the YIVO-Archive, or other important Jewish archives produced information about his later life. Subsequently I wrote to a number of people in the United States with the surname Littner compiled from various address lists. After a year of fruitless searching. I finally received a response from a woman in New York, who referred me to another relative, Kurt Grübler, who was to have collected material about the Littner family. After contacting Kurt Grübler, I found the entire history and life story of Jakob Littner after his emigration to the United States. I also found two copies of Jakob Littner's original manuscript, "Mein Weg durch die Nacht" (My journey through the night), containing 188 typed pages in a bound volume. The introduction of the manuscript bears the date November 9, 1945, the anniversary of the Nazi progrom in 1938. Now that I had the original manuscript in my hand, I could reconstruct the entire history of the book, which I first presented in an article, "Das Originalmanuskript zu Wolfgang Koeppens *Jakob Littners Aufzeichnungen aus einem Erdloch*," in *Colloquia Germanica* 2/99, pp. 117-35.

Jakob Littner was born in Budapest on April 17, 1883. In 1912 he moved with his wife Katharina to Munich where his children Zoltan, Hedda, and Yolan were born. Since Littner had become a Polish citizen in 1919 through his father who was born in Oswiecim (Auschwitz) in the Habsburg Empire, he was subject to the Nazi deportation law of October 28, 1938, from where he was sent back after three days, since Poland had protested the deportation. Littner had to leave Munich in 1939 and traveled to Prague at the time the German troops invaded. After a two-week stay he departed from Czechoslovakia and arrived in Krakow where he witnessed the German invasion of that city on September 4, 1939. From Krakow Littner fled with his Polish friend Janina Korngold through Lemberg and Tarnopol further East to Zaleszczyki on the Dnestr, where he observed the invasion of Soviet troops after the Hitler-Stalin-pact of August 23, 1939. On September 1, 1940, Littner moved on to Zbaracz in the Tarnopol district.

Here he witnessed the July 2, 1941, German attack on the Soviet Union and the invasion of SS troops into Eastern Galicia. Littner saw various activities of the Jewish council and its cooperation with the SS as well as activities of the Jewish and Ukrainian militias. On September 6, 1941, he observed the initial mass executions from which he escaped thanks to Janina's premonition. The largest part of the ghetto descriptions covers Aktionen, the large-scale SS raids. In these incursions up to one thousand people were haphazardly driven together in order to be taken by cattle cars to the nearby extermination camp at Belzec. Littner's report is one of the few authentic documents about the raids in the staging area of Holocaust exterminations. Littner adds new information about two, until now unknown, forays into the Zbaracz ghetto on September 9, 1942, and on November 9, 1942. According to Littner, the first raid took place on August 30, 1942. Littner learned about the existence of the nearby extermination camp at Belzec through reports from escaped Jews. According to Littner's report, there were further anti-Jewish raids in Zbaracz on September 9, 1942, October 20, 1942, November 9, 1942, and April 7, 1943. Similar to other occupants of the ghetto, Littner built an earthen bunker beneath his house. There he hid during raids and remained up to twenty-four hours. Even in the winter of 1942–43, when Littner became severely ill, he stayed in the bunker during times of danger.

Jakob Littner was preoccupied with the fate of his relatives in Borszczow, Hungary, and his son Zoltan in the Warsaw ghetto, who were murdered in 1942. The desperate letters of the dying Zoltan comprise the most moving documents in Littner's report. On January 8, 1943, his former business partner and companion, Christine Hintermaier, appeared in Zbaracz. She came there under the most difficult circumstances and was shocked by the prevailing living conditions inside the ghetto. Her visit is without question one of the highlights of the entire text, as it contrasts a "normal" German with the animal-like living conditions of the Jews in the ghetto. As a result, Christine became the most important person in Littner's life since he could not have survived without her assistance. This consisted of many packages and letters of comfort. The food supply helped them in their daily struggle for survival in Zbaracz, and the later supply of money made it possible for him to persuade a Polish aristocrat to provide shelter for him and Janina inside his cellar.

A new action took place in Zbaracz on April 7, 1943, after which only about nine hundred of the former five thousand Jews were still alive. Upon the conclusion of this action, Littner felt certain that the Nazis intended to empty this town of its Jews as quickly as possible. Overcome by despair, he started to look for new hiding places, since the primitive bunker beneath his house was not safe any longer. At virtually the last minute, Mr. Lachwicki, the Polish baker, sent him to the Polish land owner

Bestetzky in whose basement Jakob Littner and Janina Korngold could hide by paying him a large sum of money. All remaining inhabitants of the ghetto were killed on June 8, 1943, the day after Jakob Littner's miraculous escape.

Janina, Jakob, and later Richard Korngold remained in their underground hideout for nine months. The cruelest detail about his dark subbasement existence is the account of removing a gold tooth from his mouth. This was done to supply Bestetzky with money since Christine's mail was often stolen. Jakob Littner's subhuman existence came to an end on March 6, 1944. The report ends with his return to Munich, after having married Janina in Krakow on June 26, 1945. After returning to Munich in August 1945, the Littners lived with Christine Hintermaier. In New York, the Littners at first resided at 41st Avenue in Queens and then bought a house in Corona Heights where they lived until Jakob Littner's death on May 6, 1950. He was buried in the Beth David cemetery in Elmont, Long Island, New York. Part of this cemetery is maintained by a foundation of people who had been oppressed in Zbaracz. When Littner's daughter Yolan Grey visited Munich in 1969 she had no desire to visit Christine Hintermaier in her "flourishing" store at the Stachus. She presumed that Christine's wealth derived from Littner's original stock of postage stamps. Janina Littner died October 15, 1978. Richard Korngold still lives in New York.

Jakob Littner's "Mein Weg durch die Nach" is more complex than Koeppen's slim German volume, and it served as a basis for Kurt Grübler's work, entitled *Journey Through the Night*. Littner's "Mein Weg durch die Nacht" is without doubt one of the most impressive documents in Holocaust literature. With its detailed descriptions it testifies to future generations and is seen as a memorial to all those who perished in the Polish/Ukrainian town of Zbaracz. The precise and extensive description of the cruelties he experienced and of various events reported to him represents the best achievement of his account.

The largest part of his report includes an account of SS atrocities perpetrated against Jews. We notice Littner's attempt to represent the relationship between the SS soldiers and the Jewish residents in an episodic manner: a good example is the murder of the Jew Hindes. When the Jewish businessman Hindes declared that he no longer had the key for the storage room, he was reprimanded by the soldiers. Littner's terse description portrays the cold-blooded terror devised by SS soldiers:

> A SS soldier who confronted him insisted on confiscating the keys to his
> storeroom. Mr. Hindes explained that these had previously been taken
> away by the Soviet authorities. While the furious SS man reviled him in a

vicious manner two of his comrades were attracted by the scolding. One of
them then drew his pistol and shot Mr. Hindes at close range. After having
done so he lit a cigarette and calmly continued his conversation.
(Littner/Grübler, 24–25).

The strongest impression "Mein Weg durch die Nacht" leaves is Littner's unshak-
able faith in God through whom he accepted his destiny and his conviction that he
could endure every torment. This principle is already found in his introduction where
he points out "that God in his great kindness makes things happen that are close to
miracles where our reason has to stop. And finally, that faith in God plays an important role in overcoming seemingly inescapable situations. True faith in God creates a
strong sense of security and superhuman strength" (Littner/Grübler, 1). Early on
Littner speaks about souls of the deceased who accuse us and admonish mankind to
reconsider the uppermost sense of human dignity. These souls warn the living to
respect the life of others and leave changes in creation to God. Over and over Littner
reminds himself that he was able to endure due to his belief in the Almighty and his
trust in God's providence. He is convinced that his family will be spared during the
fateful final days of the ghetto. In this dramatic situation he leaves himself completely
to God's care: "Professor Halpern asked: 'How will our just God save us?' I replied:
'This is the creator's big secret which we mortals cannot comprehend.' I struggled
instinctively to retain my deep-rooted trust in the justness of our creator while suffering from being submerged in degradation and gloom" (Littner/Grübler, 81–82).
The story ends with a long prayer of thanksgiving to God: "Emotions of great rejoicing caused me to be almost speechless. Tears flowed freely as we thanked God for his
benevolence." Littner's story is a true salvation story: a combination of God's power
and human assistance.

His account of a subterranean existence is probably the most moving part of his
report and shows indications of dexterous linguistic abilities, especially when
Littner attempts to describe his own feelings. Even here Littner saw positive sides
and, short of shying away from praising God for this trial, describes his journey in
a mystical manner: "The prevailing silence inside our enclosure caused me to
descend ever deeper into an abyss of inertia. This enforced banishment under the
earth's surface provided an opportunity to become engrossed in somber reflections" (Littner/Grübler, 87). The somberness of this basement atmosphere contrasts sharply with the poetic description of his reemergence. He moves from a
purely scenic to a more emotional nature description: "As soon as I encountered

the sun a great feeling of emotion surged through my brain and all I could say was: 'Oh, the sun!' Indeed the bright rays now illuminated a beautiful snow scene in all directions" (Littner/Grübler, 99).

Koeppen's account of *Jakob Littners Aufzeichnungen aus einem Erdloch* as a novel turns out to be a fabrication since his narration follows minutely Jakob Littner's "Mein Weg durch die Nacht." Koeppen invented far less than we were supposed to believe; he shortened the text and expanded other parts. Since he can no longer be questioned, it is hard to determine what might have caused him to deviate from an honest account of this matter. It is evident that Koeppen used Littner's story like a quarry—he only made use of those episodes that contained poetic power. He added nothing except at the ending, but condensed several episodes and rendered Littner's description in a more literary manner. Thus, in the beginning of the text he speaks of Gestapo policemen who resembled mysterious armored beetles. They stood on guard at the potato field next to the train near the Polish border in the pale light of the rising sun (Koeppen, 21). Besides such almost Kafkaesque images, we also find images drawn from European mythology such as a description of the explosion of a bridge "like the horrible stroke of death on our backs" (Koeppen, 45). This is presented as an anticipation of the end, the eventual fate of mankind at this time; to burrow into the ground, or to hide oneself from vultures. Man no longer participates in the dream of Icarus—Koeppen's symbol for human progress. Koeppen's image of SS men in white coats, who appear more terrible than ghosts, is even stronger. They are "ogres," who demand their tribute in human flesh, "messengers of hell" of a civilization gone insane (Koeppen, 76). Later Koeppen introduces the medieval Dance of Death where people are mowed down with machine guns (Koeppen, 117). Upon termination of the raids the few remaining Jews appear to Koeppen as though they were fish in a pool.

The structure of Koeppen's text indicates a concentration upon death images. This symbolic structure may be compared to the structure of the content, which describes Littner's fate within ever tighter concentric circles. Most of Koeppen's symbols represent natural phenomena against which Littner's struggle appears to be futile right from the start. While Littner and his fellow Jews are portrayed as human beings, SS soldiers are depersonalized as demons. Myths and symbols are expressions of a considerably greater evil, which overpowers mankind at this time ("It is a bad time"; "It is a dark century"; "The flame of war was burning"; "Robbery, murder and rape came upon us like the weather"; "The brown house expanded like a cancer"). All of these symbols are designed to prepare each individual for the inevitable experience of dying into an all-embracing event which may be regarded as being part of a historical event seen in the European context of distress. Thus the experience of Littner's suffering is deprived of its singularity and elevated to a more common level. Littner's unmistakable victim-culprit relationship is elevated to a mythical level. Finally, the SS butchers are absolved of their guilt while the victims are absolved of their suffering.

Koeppen displays a tendency to emphasize the role of "good Germans." While it is true that Littner described Christine's efforts for his survival as well as the initially benign atmosphere after the German occupation of Zbaracz, Koeppen invents additional sympathy between Littner and the good Germans, most of whom opposed the killings and destruction of Kristallnacht (Koeppen, 29). These remarks are topped only by Koeppen's praise of the first commandant in Zbaracz: "How desirable it would be if all German masters were like this one. We would race through the countryside and give away our last belongings" (Koeppen, 34). This final passage contradicts the whole attitude of Littner's memories. He does not wish to depend upon the Germans as "masters," but wants to determine his fate by himself alone.

Koeppen's possible motivation for his alterations becomes more evident in a two-page summary and interpretation of events, which differs from the rest of the text. While Littner described the hanged SS gendarme Jetzt as "deeply moving," Koeppen's Littner does not know what do with the functionaries of murder. There can be no punishment which would restore the murder victims to life and thereby nullify the injustice. Since justice has ceased to exist in this world one must at last stop the killing, since sentencing SS members to death would only be an act of vengeance, but not justice. It seems that for Koeppen the question of guilt played a central role in his writing, and this could have been the prime motive for compiling this book. He compares the Germans with the lost Jews and adds his rather naïve thoughts to the effect that had most Germans acted decently Nazi power would have collapsed. Littner declares that hatred is a dreadful expression that caused inhuman events to take place; he believes that he did not have a single enemy in Munich. Koeppen, however, states that the German people's guilt can only be judged by God. Koeppen picks up Littner's declaration from his introduction that he does not intend to promote hatred, an amazing concept coming from a Jew in 1945. Thus, Koeppen's final rejection of hatred exists in Littner's text, although Koeppen places it in a more prominent place at the very end: "Hatred is a terrible word. Hatred, lunacy and stupidity brought this misery upon us. . . . Only God can judge" (Koeppen, 149).

Kurt Grübler's translation and edition of the Littner text is the first time it appears in English. Grübler expanded Littner's report with his own research. Grübler also added a number of historic and personal documents to Littner's text, and this provides it with more historical significance. Grübler also made use of information that derived from interviews he conducted with Littner's daughter Yolan Grey and with Richard Korngold (set in italics and within brackets in the text proper) along with various sources from the United States Holocaust Museum (placed in the endnotes). While these texts tend to slightly encroach upon the diary's usefulness in regard to Littner's report, they help to establish historical accuracy that was badly missing in Koeppen's text. Consequently, it is now possible to classify Koeppen's text as an elaborate fictionalization of authentic events where the dividing line between truth and fantasy remains blurred (see Wilkomirski). Kurt Grübler provides a more detailed account not only of Littner's experiences, but also of the bigger historical picture. The host of documents, relating to the Littner family, greatly enhances the historical objectivity of his book.

Reinhard K. Zachau

Preface

I, Kurt Grübler, was born on September 16, 1925, in Vienna, Austria. My paternal grandfather, Nathan, born in 1842, derived from the locality of Rajsko near the town of Auschwitz, located in the former Austrian province of Galicia. He was married to Anna Littner, his niece, and similar to many other Galician Jews they came to establish residency in the imperial metropolis of Vienna. There he owned a shoe manufacturing enterprise located at the inner city's Wachtelgasse next to the Fischerstiege. Nathan, accompanied by his wife and daughter, Julia, embarked upon a voyage to New York in 1890. When my father, David Grübler, was born they lived at 295 East 3rd Street in 1892.

Nathan Grübler together with his wife and two children returned to Vienna in 1898. There they resided at Rueppgasse inside the Leopoldstadt district. David attended school in the Blumauergasse. His older sister embarked upon a dancing career. Nathan's sickly wife, Anna, succumbed to a heart attack in 1902. Then Nathan sent his young son David to Budapest to live with Sigmund Littner, one of his uncles. David Grübler returned to Vienna in 1913 and at the start of the first World War in 1914 he joined the Austrian army. He soon found himself at the eastern front as a common soldier.

He was captured by the Russians together with others and remained in Siberian captivity until the Russian empire collapsed in 1917. Upon returning to Budapest he learned that his father had died in 1915 at the Jewish old age home in Vienna.

My mother, Josefa Heiss, born a Catholic in March 1899 in Vienna, converted to Judaism upon marrying my father. She had a diploma as a clothing designer and worked in that capacity.

I vividly recall the widespread condition of poverty as it prevailed during the years of economic depression, accompanied by violent political conflicts. While the Austrian government tried to cope with this destabilizing situation I followed the example of other Jewish youngsters and joined the Zionist movement in 1935. This was the socialist-oriented Gordonia and I remained in its summer encampment in Lower Austria. Later, I and several of my friends joined the ranks of the militant organization known as Betar. Inspired by Vladimir Jabotinsky, the Zionist activist, it espoused a militant approach to solving the existing "Jewish Problem."

Four months after the Austrian republic's demise in 1938, my father succeeded in obtaining an American passport. He took me and my younger sister to New York, but my mother had to wait four more months until she was allowed to join us.

The arduous task of compiling *Journey Through the Night* serves as my contribution to the already existing large volume of holocaust literature. The recounted events should serve to enlighten future generations about the dreadful events that occurred during the supposedly advanced twentieth century. The depicted happenings were recorded by Mr. Jakob Littner in his memoirs. He was related to my father and both men spent their maturing years in Budapest.

Mr. Richard Korngold, Jakob Littner's stepson, rendered vital aid to my exertions by providing first-hand information about Jakob Littner's complicated life in Munich, their common frightening experiences inside the Zbaracz ghetto, as well as his final years of relative comfort while living in New York City.

Mr. Korngold kindly provided me with additional information concerning his own life. He also gave me Mr. Littner's original manuscript together with photographs, drawings, letters, and postcards. I recently took it upon myself to visit the Polish city of Krakow where I interviewed people at the old Korngold-Littner residence whose memory still lingered on there.

Kurt Nathan Grübler

Editor's Note

Jakob Littner was born in Budapest, Hungary, in 1883, the oldest of five children, three sons and two daughters. A graduate, at the age of 18, of the Hungarian-Israelite Agricultural and Industrial Trade Association, Littner moved to Munich in 1912, with his wife, Katherine. There they had three children, a son, Zoltan, and two daughters, Hedda and Yolan. In Munich Littner initially acquired a stationary store. Eventually, he owned a profitable philatelic business, with a partner, a Christian woman by the name of Christine Hintermeyer. It was located in the heart of Munich, near the National Socialist Workers Party Headquarters. At some point during these years Littner and his wife separated. Suffering bouts of depression, Katherine returned to her parents in Budapest, where she spent many of the remaining years of her life in a sanatorium until she was killed by the Nazis in 1944. The Littners' daughters, Yolan and Hedda, had immigrated to the United States in 1937.

Although Jakob Littner had been born in Budapest and had lived there until migrating to Munich in 1912, he was considered a Polish national through his father, David, who had been born in Galicia, an Austrian province, which had become Polish after Poland gained its independence in 1919. Thus, in October of 1938, when Hitler planned to expel some 50,000 Jews with Polish passports, Littner was among them. Upon his expulsion from the German Reich, Littner found temporary refuge in Krakow. When German troops invaded Poland, Littner, together with his landlady, Janina Korngold, and her two sons, Mietek and Richard, fled eastward, where they eventually settled in Zbaracz, a locality near Tarnopol.

In August 1945, after the harrowing events described in this memoir, Littner returned to Munich with Janina Korngold, now his wife, and her son Richard. Here he wrote his report which he finished on November 9, 1945, the anniversary of Crystal Night. Littner's story is one of the first Holocaust memoirs available. In

November 1946, Richard immigrated to the United States, followed shortly by Littner and Janina, who arrived in New York on July 17, 1947. The Littners eventually settled in the Corona section of Queens, where Littner died in his sleep on May 6, 1950, at 67 years of age. He was interred in a parcel of land owned by the Zbaracz Relief Society in the Beth David Cemetery in Elmhurst. Janina lived for another twenty-eight years with her son Richard in Flushing. She died at 87 on October 15, 1978.

Introduction

There are two reasons why I decided to write the following report. First, I wanted to show that good and evil are close together on this earth and that the brightest light of good spreads to the darkest shadows of evil. The principle of evil does not have its home with a single people as false propaganda has taught for a long time, a false doctrine that inflicted a truly hypnotic effect on people and by which horrible misery came into this world. Furthermore I want to state that God in his great kindness makes things happen that are close to miracles where our reason has to stop. And finally, that faith in God plays an important role in overcoming seemingly inescapable situations. True faith in God creates a strong sense of security and superhuman strength.

Secondly, I considered it my holy duty to set a memorial to all those countless and nameless individuals and all those who have shown us their honorable intentions in helping the poor souls. Unknown are the graves of most who perished; there are no grave stones or signs about their suffering and their end. Thus the present report shall be dedicated to the memory of all those who perished.

The facts in this report and in the reported letters are authentic. In addition, the thousands still living in Zbaracz can confirm these facts at any time. The picture I portray is only part of my experiences. The complete report of everything would cover volumes.

It is not the task of this report to foster hatred, or to report sensations. I have been attacked in the past when I forgave a hostile person his intentions and actions. It is not for people to judge others! It is my hope that all, no matter of what religion, will forgive each other!

There is only one God. I myself can not make a difference between individuals of different faiths and I always delight in true faith in God. True believers are incapable of the monstrous actions that happened.

May the souls of the poor victims rest in peace. May the poor tortured world find the peace that it badly needs in order to give mankind back its decency! I hope that I have made a small contribution toward bringing mankind back together again.

Jakob Littner
Munich, November 9, 1945

[1]

In 1912 I moved from Budapest to Munich. We found a country with deep-rooted peace, lucky Bavaria, splendid people! One had to like it there, where the hearty "Grüß Gott" was used. What profound and beautiful meaning had the Bavarian motto "Live and let live"! But how would this motto be violated to the cruelest extreme only a quarter century later! The Bavarian idyll of comfortable and tolerant joy of life remains unforgettable. After a few short happy years it was disturbed and the shining white and blue sky lost its shine.

World War I overshadowed the country. Misery and suffering came over the people and their spiritual stability was largely shaken. This was the appropriate breeding ground for the germination of a political direction of intolerance, violence, and ethnic hatred, whose consequences would later shake up the entire world to an unheard-of extent.

I myself attempted to master the postwar period with diligence and endurance, but the shadows of things to come loomed over all my efforts. Especially the lunacy of racial hatred was soon upon us with an intensity that would have been worthy of a much more noble goal. I cannot say how many small humiliations, gibes, and hidden aggressions we had to endure. But it seemed impossible then that these systematic hatred campaigns would ever cause much of a problem in Germany. We looked for consolation and diversion in our work.

But the pressure became still stronger. The political anarchism that developed at that time was exploited unscrupulously by those elements whose major attribute was envy. Requests for police hearings were issued. They became more common. I was summoned due to accusations of a ridiculous nature; yes, they even wanted to take a picture of me there. I protested that I was no criminal. Only the intervention of my attorney, Dr. Schwink, achieved the retraction of this accusation.

On an October morning in 1938 at 5 A.M. a uniformed policeman appeared in my apartment, got me out of bed, and said after checking my papers, "I have to arrest you." I was given no explanation as to why I was arrested. I was only allowed to call my business partner, Christine H. She appeared soon with her sister, and I was allowed to give her my keys and money. Then I was taken to the police station. There my passport was confiscated, but I still did not know what was going on. I did not remain alone for long. Continuously more people were brought in, among them children still with their schoolbags; they had been arrested in school. As I found out later, their parents had been taken to other police stations. Slowly the ward filled up. We were mostly Jews with Polish citizenship papers.

I am a Polish citizen through the fact that my father was born in Auschwitz. But as a 13-year-old boy he settled in Hungary. Auschwitz, which is known throughout the world today, is no longer a simple geographic name, it has become a symbol! When I used to mention Auschwitz, nobody knew where it was located until it had become so notoriously famous.

After some time an old woman with her daughter and son-in-law came into the ward. Since he was a non-Jew, he could leave the station. I used this opportunity to inform my partner of the fact that I had been arrested and at which police station I was located. Hours upon hours passed in the meantime and the room became unbearably packed, so that nobody could move any more. Children began to cry, some old people fainted, and the situation became increasingly unpleasant. Around 11 A.M. a policeman came and told me that my attorney, Dr. Schwink, wanted to talk to me. Under supervision of a policeman I could exchange a few words with him. Despite the presence of the policeman, I was able to say to my attorney secretly: "Look in this room and see the misery!" It was important to me to speak to my attorney and find out from him that it was not a personal measure directed against me, but a general decree to expel all Polish-Jewish citizens. Dr. Schwink had found out about my arrest through my business partner, and he had contacted the Polish consulate immediately. Christine, as I will call her from now on, had prepared a small suitcase with food supplies for me. Dr. Schwink brought the case along. I, of course, shared the content of the suitcase with my fellow prisoners and soon sausage, rolls, and vermouth wine were eaten up and drunk completely. All of these people were in an understandable state of excitement, since they had been torn so suddenly from their familiar surroundings. In some cases they had been separated from relatives who mostly did not know why they had been arrested. I could inform them now of what I knew and I tried to comfort every one according to my ability.

Around 4 P.M. we were finally loaded on trucks and taken out of the city. We were deposited at the gate of Stadelheim Prison. There was a big crowd of people. Around a thousand people must have been brought there from various police stations. We were taken through a number of courtyards and gates, which were immediately closed behind us. Finally we arrived at a long and wide hallway which housed a row of single cells. Some of the guards were correct, others compassionate, several rude and violent. They pushed the people forward with their fists and did not hide their hatred toward us. When everyone who had been brought here was in the room, they divided us into groups of two or three and sent us to the cells. There we waited for things to come. We were prepared to spend the night. In the meantime the Jewish community had acted on our behalf in an exemplary manner. They sent a delegation, and a leader gave a short speech from which we learned that we would be moved on the following morning at 3 A.M. Furthermore we had the opportunity to obtain necessary clothing and other items from our apartments through these friends. We only had to give them our keys, and then a suitcase was packed for everyone with the most important items and taken to the station the following morning.

After the delegation had left, we prepared for the night as well as we could. We were also given coffee and bread. The remaining guards behaved in a human manner, some even played with the children. We noticed that the children and the older people were getting tired, and they lay down on the wooden beds trying to sleep. Most of us, however, spent the night in the hall shivering and pondering our fate; some of us were engaged in unpleasant conversations conducted in low voices. Outside a cold fall rain fell and slowly, very slowly, one hour passed after another. A little aside a group of Jews, which I joined, gathered for prayer.

At 3 A.M. everything had to be ready. We received coffee and bread, then we descended to the courtyard. At 5 A.M. the prison doors opened and we were led outside through a row of policemen to the waiting buses, which took us to the station. There we were again taken through rows of policemen to the waiting train. It was interesting that hardly an onlooker dared to move closer; they only looked furtively from a distance. We had the impression that these people neither knew the cause of our arrest nor agreed with it. But they themselves were obviously so frightened that they displayed an air of indifference which excluded a spontaneous expression of their opinion. And yet this was only the beginning of a terrible development!

To us expellees this future appeared rather gloomy and it must have been good that most of us only vaguely comprehended what was in store for us. Only a few of those unfortunate ones may still be alive.

At the station a suitcase with the necessary belongings was waiting for everyone. In selfless labor the Munich Jewish community had collected the luggage from the homes of the expellees. They had also provided sausage, bread, bananas, and other food items, even socks for some of us. All of this helped us to endure our fate more easily. We bade farewell with many words of thanks and with best wishes for the ones staying behind.

Time passed and the train rolled on and on. Where to? Nobody could tell. A policeman was sitting at every exit, where he was relieved every two hours. We stopped in Augsburg and Nuremberg, where more Jews boarded the train; we saw more tears and intense suffering.

The gray, unfriendly fall day was not suited to lifting our depressed mood. In many of us the shock of the sudden deportation and its brutal execution showed itself with a nervous reaction. By a lucky coincidence, a Munich doctor and a nurse accompanied our transport. They had a lot to do. We again owed this act of mercy to the Munich Jewish community.

More food was not provided during the transport. Those who had something could eat; the others were not forgotten by the lucky ones with food. Everybody took special care of the children. A serious problem, however, were the mothers with babies. Where could we find milk, especially warm milk? Even the adults suffered from thirst since we lacked water. I myself did not eat a bite.

On our trip through the gray landscape, I started a conversation with the policeman sitting next to me. He wanted me to know that he felt sorry for us. This humanly acting policeman also promised to visit Christine upon his return to Munich and report to her where we had gone. It was a great comfort to me to talk to him. At least during our conversation I did not have to pursue the gloomy thoughts that forced themselves upon me. When the friendly policeman was relieved every two hours by a colleague, who acted unpleasantly, everything got grayer. I was glad when the friendly policeman came back again.

A glance into the car behind us showed me that it was a special car. Gestapo people were sitting at long tables with radio equipment.

Night came upon us, the time when two days before we could have turned on the light in our comfortable homes. And now this sudden change! The last part of our trip continued through darkness. At midnight our policeman came back. He told me secretly: "I believe that you will go free." I noticed his joy in being able to tell me that. Suddenly the train stopped on a field near the Polish border. It took a while and then we heard the Gestapo men scream outside: "From each car one Jew out!" Their way of addressing us was always "You Jew" or "You Jewess." We complied with their request, and it took a long time again until our delegates came back to report. They had been told that the Polish government had objected to our expulsion and that we would have to return to Munich on the same train, at our own expense however, which would be 7.80 marks per person.

Our joy was indescribable. Some cried, most cheered, and everyone was happy; nobody noticed the pitch dark night any longer, nobody felt the hunger, thirst, or cold. Everybody forgot about the cramped quarters in the train car. We could go home again! We collected the money immediately. We also took up a collection for the poorer Jews, which resulted in a great success. Thus the train began moving back to Munich. Since everything related to dirt has been connected by evil propaganda with us Jews, we agreed to leave every train car in such immaculate state that not even a scrap of paper could assault the eye of a fanatic Jew-hater.

It was at 9 P.M. when we were back at Munich's main train station. Again the Jewish community had done us a service. People delegated by them stood ready at the platform in order to carry the luggage of those returning. Cars had been procured and most of us were taken back to our homes. Aside from the already mentioned offenses, we did not have to endure anything worse in the days to come.

Then came November 9, 1938![1]

On this "holiday" we did not want to stay home due to the riots that were certainly expected. We spent the day outside the city alone and returned late in the evening. At the station we saw the posted telegraph notice with the headline: "Ernst vom Rath died from his wounds!"

I returned to my apartment. At that time I had a living arrangement with the Kruger family. When I entered, I noticed Mr. Kr. was listening to the news on radio in the company of three other gentlemen. After our welcome I expressed my fears regarding the coming night. "But no, Littner, it will probably not be so bad for you." This and other comforting remarks could not dispel my fears, and consequently I could not find any sleep. In my pondering I was interrupted about 3 A.M. by the telephone ringing. I heard Kr. say on the phone "No, I do not want to tell him!"

Upon my probing questions he told me that riots had been reported to him. Jewish businesses had been ransacked, the synagogue had been burned, and my own business had been destroyed. Shortly thereafter the three mentioned friends came back and advised me to hide; it would be better for me. In the meantime Christine, whom I had informed by telephone, went to the store and saw the destruction herself. Glass debris together with the window display was scattered all over the sidewalk and the street. The precious interior of our nice store was a total mess.

What hurt Christine most was the behavior of a business colleague by the name of Riess; this cynical man paraded with impertinent gestures in front of our destroyed business. One could see his pleasure and gloating. It was hard to believe that R. just happened to come by our store at such an early hour.

I fled by cab to Laim where my friends Luchs and Frau Hedwig Gründl sheltered me; they were both very worried about me. It was through me that they first heard about the events of the night; they comforted me and insisted that I stay with them. They wanted to shelter and feed me. In the meantime I phoned Christine to tell her about my new hiding place.

I felt happy in the comfortable rooms of their pleasant villa. Their hospitality did me very well, but I could not enjoy this nice rest for long. At 7 A.M. the next morning Frau Gr. appeared suddenly and told me in an excited and timid manner that SS units were already searching nearby houses in order to find hidden Jews. Thus I was forced to depart again. After a warm farewell from my friends I found myself on the street, prey for my persecutors. Everywhere I could see policemen with arrested Jews, some without a coat or hat, but a merciful destiny prevented me from the same fate at that time. Like a pursued criminal, I had to hide in the Landsberger Straße behind an old building. At an appropriate moment I sneaked to a close-by phone booth and informed Christine about the events, as well as about my current hiding place. After an endless and anxious waiting period when I could have been arrested any minute, Christine, my good spirit, appeared and we started walking in the direction of the train station. When the streets became more crowded, she ran in front of me since she as a non-Jew could not be seen with me.

I noticed yellow signs on all stores, even pharmacies, with the text: "Jews not admitted!" All Jewish stores had been destroyed. The synagogue was still burning. This had been a well-prepared work of destruction and not the discharge of "spontaneous public rage" as the Nazis had maintained.

Finally Christine arrived with a car. My luck was that I could at least temporarily hide from my persecutors in a corner of this car. The only chance for safety was the Polish consulate. I remembered the dentist Dr. N., a friend of mine, who was also in danger. We first went to his apartment where I saved him by taking him along to the Polish consulate, where he could hide as well. As we later found out from his wife, the police came to their house soon afterwards to arrest him. They searched the house and confiscated various things. His escape saved him from Dachau, where all apprehended Jews had been taken at that time.

The Polish consulate was filled to capacity with refugees. Even with our official protection by the Polish government we still lived in terrible uncertainty. For many days after November 9 we still had to hide in Munich. Lest we starve, our savior Christine brought us food secretly. The situation was quite dangerous for her. We ourselves could not buy anything. In general, the golden unspoiled heart of many inhabitants of Munich showed itself again. How much secret assistance was rendered! We heard from many Jews that they found food, milk, and bread secretly placed in front of their doors. They were assisted in this and similar ways. This needs to be stated here with emphasis in order to do justice to the many honorable people in Munich.

After we had left the Polish consulate, since we still did not dare to return to our homes, we found refuge with the furrier family H., who lived opposite Munich's Hofbrauhaus, where we spent the night sitting in a small room. Beneath us was a small cafe where the pianist was playing almost the same tune from the early morning hours till late at night. The following day we still had to stay quietly in this room since the employees of the furrier family worked in the adjoining room. For another few days we were forced to hide with several other families until we could feel safer again in the city.

Despite this assistance we also had to endure much hatred. The beast in man shows itself often enough on those occasions. The already mentioned R., a businessman in my field, distinguished himself particularly. This man whom I had aided in the past began to connive against me, supported by some similar-thinking people, not only against me but also against Christine, and that in a particularly nasty manner. Christine would have a lot of trouble because of him.

We got by with difficulty, as outcasts and barely tolerated members of society, not safe for a single moment. In addition, the rules and restrictions concerning Jews became ever more strict. Now non-Jewish home-owners were no longer allowed to house a Jew. I was thus forced to change my apartment. I could do nothing but move to Dr. N.'s house.

My store remained closed and I could no longer enter it. It was also off-limits to Christine although both of us tried to gain permission to continue the business. After months of waiting we finally obtained permission to enter the store in order to finalize the ownership transfer, although the noble Mr. R. fought it violently even with a list of signatures. He wanted to prevent Christine from keeping the business since he wanted it for himself. After all that had happened I no longer enjoyed my business; but, nevertheless, I needed to take care of Christine, since she had contributed so much to the success of our business with her selfless manner.

My daughters, Yolan and Hedwig, who suffered from emotional distress in Munich, took advantage of an opportunity to emigrate to the United States. I also applied for an immigrant's visa at the American consulate in Stuttgart but destiny steered me in a very different direction. On February 15, 1939, I received a summons to appear at police headquarters. Upon arrival at the appointed hour an officer who handled my case stated bluntly: "It is my unpleasant duty to present you with bad news. It has been decided that you must remove yourself from the German Reich within fourteen days. You may request a review of the case but I must tell you right now that it will do you no good." In reply to my question whether I had broken a law or done something wrong, he answered: "No, absolutely nothing. All cases concerning foreign Jewish residents are handled in a similar manner."

Having been born and raised in Hungary, I communicated with its representation in Germany and asked for permission to return home. My application was rejected since repatriation was not desired at that time even though my brother, Lajos, together with my sisters, Irma and Sida, offered to protect me. Then a former acquaintance who now lived in London declared that he was willing to shelter me but his efforts on my behalf bore no fruit. Eventually I succeeded in obtaining a Czechoslovakian visa which limited my stay in that country to three months.

[2]

On March 1, 1939, I left Munich, on a train bound for Prague, with ten Reichsmark in my pocket and a piece of hand luggage filled with spare clothes. Several fellow passengers with Polish passports sought to reach the same destination. At the border several SS officers came to inspect passports. They asked routine questions and after stamping the vital documents returned them to their owners. As soon as the train left the station and crossed over into the still free country, I felt greatly relieved. Upon my arrival in Prague, I stood next to the terminal not knowing where to go. My wallet contained just enough money to hire a taxi to convey me to a cheap hotel. The next day, in order to obtain additional funds, I sold various sets of stamps that were in my possession to a dealer. I began to nurture dim hopes of being allowed to remain temporarily in Prague. People whom I encountered complained about the strident German propaganda directed against their country.

Since it was evident that bad times would soon descend upon this republic, I thought it best to move on. I obtained a Portuguese visa as well as a transit visa for France, but newly issued regulations forced me to give up this venture. A depressive mood descended upon the citizens of Prague, and by March 14 it turned into a panic. Most hotel guests stayed awake during the night, and the news that German troops were about to enter Prague reached us at five o'clock in the morning. Later that sad day I went to the Wenzelsplatz where I encountered a very large crowd consisting mostly of *Volksdeutsche* (ethnic Germans). These elated people gathered there to welcome long lines of German soldiers. This great rectangular square abounded with civilians who, in accordance with the current Nazi fashion, wore white stockings. The unhappy Czechs remained mostly in the side streets, and many of them shed bitter tears of despair. It is hard for me to describe the prevailing emotional scenes. Upon my return to the hotel I discovered that it was already requisitioned by German officers. Jewish guests were ordered to vacate the premises by three o'clock in the afternoon.

11

I quickly packed my suitcase and with passport in hand dashed over to the train station. There, while encountering an excited crowd of people, I succeeded in boarding an express train at almost the last minute. It went to Maerisch-Ostrau and then on into Poland.

In Poland I encountered a perplexing situation upon arrival at the border. An official who examined my Polish passport berated me for not being able to answer his question in Polish. Since I already knew where I wished to go, the confrontation did not disturb me. My immediate destination was Bielitz where many Jews from Germany had found a temporary place of refuge. Several remote relatives of mine lived there as well. After having reached Bielitz I gained some badly needed rest in a boarding house, and then on Friday evening I visited the local synagogue. This sanctuary appeared to be crowded with worshippers. Among them were many refugees who praised God for having been provided with a place of refuge. The dignity of ongoing devotional services impressed me greatly. While sitting there, tears flowed from my eyes. Since I had endured so much adversity in Munich, intermittent sobs convulsed my body. While praising God I could not anticipate the violence that still awaited me. Here I encountered Jews who, while longing for the good times in Germany, said: "Life used to be better there. It was more efficient and orderly." I too thought about Munich and its many attractions until receiving information about the barbaric actions carried out against helpless people.

Since my destination happened to be Krakow, I remained in Bielitz for only a short time. Even though my son, Zoltan, had already joined the Polish army, I knew that he and his wife, Rosalia, were living in Krakow. It is difficult to describe the feeling of joy that overwhelmed me while thinking of seeing their faces. I anticipated my imminent arrival in Krakow with suspense and went from the terminal directly to their home. Zoltan also awaited my arrival with impatience. He wore a new uniform and it fitted him well. He had become a dashing soldier of whom I could be very proud.

I wanted to find a more permanent accommodation. By chance someone recommended me to the owner of an apartment who wished to rent out one room. I quickly went to the given address at Lobsovska Street 43 to be interviewed. The woman whom I met was a Mrs. Janina Korngold, a widow who had graduated from Krakow university. She lived with two sons, named Richard, thirteen, and Mietek, seventeen years of age. I gladly accepted the terms of rental for a comfortably furnished room and quickly moved in with my lone suitcase. I congratulated myself for having found a nice place amidst congenial surroundings.

Since my son, Zoltan, was obliged to rejoin his army unit by August 1, 1939, I devoted much time to him. Soon I accompanied him to the railroad station where we embraced and exchanged a final handshake. Zoltan entered a passenger car, and as the train started to move he waved to me. A sudden feeling of distress overwhelmed me since my only son now faced a most uncertain future. He waved for a long time, with sadness, as if he anticipated his fate.

While relying upon the assurances of Mrs. Korngold, I looked forward to a restoration of my emotional balance. Christine, the faithful soul, responded quickly to my letters by sending money and sets of postage stamps. Once she surprised me by telephoning to inform me about her efforts to establish contacts with my family members in Budapest.

Like many other localities, Krakow became afflicted by manifestations of tension while increasing efforts to construct defensive barriers were being launched. The large cellar in our building was quickly converted into an air-raid shelter. It had recently been furnished with camp beds and a radio receiver. Mrs. Korngold accepted the position of air-raid warden, and her implements consisted of an old bugle and a bell. Since Mrs. Korngold was destined to play a most vital role in the unfolding drama, I shall henceforth refer to her as Janina. Initially the citizens of Krakow expected an increase of tensions, but now they realized that a severe crisis was about to unfold. Indeed, what soon happened turned out to be a major disaster.

Air-raid sirens loudly announced the start of an invasion at five o'clock in the morning on September 1, 1939. We dashed down into our shelter and remained there for many hours. While peeking through a conveniently located basement window, I could easily observe German warplanes as they flew at a very low altitude. The very first day of a repeated world war had started, and now we experienced our baptism of fire. Ear-splitting noises that emanated from antiaircraft guns and exploding bombs did not abate. One bomb that landed on a nearby building caused extensive damage. Many houses soon had missing roofs while streets were covered with broken glass. Janina became one of the first casualties. She was supposed to go into action during the first alarm, but since this good woman nearly fainted she was unable to use her trumpet and bell. A roving rescue team carried her back into our shelter where eventually she recovered.

When the air attack ended, I emerged onto a balcony and observed the many raging fires amidst widespread destruction. The railroad station, having been selected as a prime target, was engulfed by flames. Soon a large number of people who had been rendered homeless sought to enter the shelter in our building. Since I had no knowledge of their language, I spoke to them in German, but they became very angry and insisted that I address them in Polish. Having no choice in this matter, I now thought it best to remain silent. Since that day of initiation we could hardly get enough sleep. Many groups of soldiers, as well as civilians who carried personal belongings tried to reach pre-assigned armories. People who sought to buy food formed long lines in front of stores. A family, having been rendered homeless, left their old and sick father in our house. We placed him on a cot in the basement and tried to nurture him, but he died a few days later.

Rumors to the effect that strong German forces were advancing toward Krakow spread rapidly while a massive flow of refugees passed through its streets. Local residents began to panic while we observed unfolding events. Those who tried to get away often carried bundles and bedding tied onto poles. Some escapees pulled carts filled with necessities as well as useful farm animals. This great movement of disoriented humanity flowed eastwards in a steady stream. The janitor of our building was an embittered woman who now thought it best to affix a picture of the Mother of God on her door. At the same time she encouraged her children to join others in ransacking the railroad yards. They returned home loaded down with boxes filled with utensils and foods.

Men who could be drafted wished to save themselves by fleeing. Janina's older son, Mietek, together with his wife, also fled from the doomed city in the company of friends on bicycles. Even though most people sought to get out of harm's way, there were those who knew that they lacked the strength to cover long distances on foot. Increasingly, large numbers of wounded and hungry Polish soldiers began to pass through. We distributed some bread and other food in front of our house to these unlucky men. Amidst this confusion German warplanes kept circling overhead, and whenever these appeared we quickly descended into our basement.

When many buildings in our vicinity began to burn, we decided to abandon the shelter. We maintained a friendly relationship with one family that owned a construction firm. Its owner often drove a large truck, which was expected to arrive in Krakow soon from Warsaw. Since German forces were closing in on the city, we found it expedient to use the truck for a headlong flight. It was the fourth of September, and setting fires as well as committing burglaries became the order of the day or, better said, night. Since city streets were no longer illuminated, nocturnal criminal elements began to dominate them. Under these dire circumstances, we got very little sleep. While violent activities occurred we could not alert the police since all guardians of law and order had by now abandoned their posts. We realized that the time for us to leave at once had arrived. After standing on guard for several nights, I fell asleep from exhaustion, and Janina had to wake me when the longed-for vehicle showed up.

We collected various necessary items in preparation for our departure. I foolishly thought that we would soon return and therefore I wore my worst clothes. Janina urged me to take along a winter coat, but the weather was quite warm and I ignored her good advice. This was a bad decision since matters turned out differently than I had imagined. Shortly before our departure, Janina took hold of a large portrait of her deceased husband. She placed it against the wall of her room, together with two burning candles on either side of the revered object. In this manner she bid farewell to the past and to her home in Krakow. The vehicle that we boarded could accommodate twenty-three people and as it moved along, its open back provided us with a clear view of the burning city. We passed the warehouse of a cigarette factory that was engulfed by flames. While fire illuminated the road ahead, pillaging mobs celebrated orgies.

It became difficult to proceed at high speed since conditions of chaos prevailed at frequently encountered obstacles. People in flight threatened to block our way while disorganized groups of soldiers converged upon us from several sides. We also halted near roadblocks where soldiers stood by to examine the vehicle. Since our truck had a military permit, it was allowed to proceed. While German aircraft flew above the traffic chaos, we often had to seek shelter off the pavement whenever danger threatened. So as to avoid being strafed by machinegun fire, we proceeded along rutted byways that caused us to be painfully shaken. Since the weather was still warm, an increasing thirst began to afflict us. Several strangers, whom we permitted to join us, refused to leave later on and we had to take them along.

During the afternoon hours we reached a pleasant village and decided to remain there so as to rest and to consume some of our provisions. At dusk we came to a place called Szczucin where the driver hid his vehicle under a cluster of broad trees, but he stayed with it in order to prevent its disappearance. Seeking shelter for the night we entered a nearby farmhouse. The owners of this place had prepared a large room to accommodate fleeing people. In its center stood a table, and sacred objects, surrounded by burning candles, had been placed on it. Our hosts also distributed generous quantities of straw throughout this room. Without receiving a formal invitation, we stretched out as we were and quickly fell asleep. The following morning—it was September 6—we prepared ourselves to continue this journey into the unknown. The kind farmer and his wife gave us a pot filled with hot milk and thick slices of bread so as to provide us with sufficient energy to move on.

Meanwhile hordes of refugees and retreating groups of soldiers began to clog the road. This situation prevented our driver from advancing at a reasonable rate of speed. In order to gain time we, the passengers, opted to proceed on foot, but soon this effort began to drain away our supply of energy. Then we came upon a bridge that spanned the Vistula river in the vicinity of Szczucin. At this site we encountered a severe bottleneck since a military police unit stood by to control the flow of traffic. Our truck soon caught up with us on the opposite shore and we quickly clambered aboard. At this point our driver was able to move ahead much faster, but then we observed German warplanes as they flew toward the bridge. Several well-aimed bombs caused the span to collapse quickly, and now the vital link to the opposite bank had ceased to exist. Our successful escape from Krakow covered, for the time being, an adequate distance. Janina felt overjoyed when she noticed a group of bycicle riders since her son, Mietek, was among them. She tried to talk him into joining us, but he declared that it would not be fair to abandon his friends. We therefore continued on our way to Warsaw without him. We rested in a small town that had already sustained considerable damage from air attacks. Still, we managed to obtain a decent noonday meal, but every so often we were forced to seek shelter. Since we wished to spend the night in a forest clearing, our flight continued until the late afternoon. Fortunately, the prolonged warm weather permitted us to do so. At dawn, while enemy planes resumed their strafing activities, we began to move with care. Those whom we came across traveling in the opposite direction told us that many people in Warsaw had also abandoned their homes. This disturbing report convinced us to change our plans and head for Lvov (Lemberg) instead.

Along the way we encountered several burning dwellings, and then our driver ran out of fuel. Fortunately, he acquired a large enough quantity from a nearby village. This supply enabled us to advance a certain distance until the fuel gave out once again while on the open road. The next morning enough gasoline was brought to us by bycicle from a greater distance. Due to these unavoidable delays, we finally arrived in Lvov at a late hour on September 9. We obtained lodgings from the family of Professor Katz, who happened to be an acquaintance of Janina. The family members consisted of the professor, his wife, daughter, and mother-in-law. They all welcomed us most graciously. The entire family was later murdered. Fred, Janina's brother, who also escaped from Krakow at almost the last moment, brought along Janina's younger son, Richard, with his car. They all arrived safely at the Katz residence. Early next morning we debated about our direction of flight. Everyone agreed that the most expedient move would be toward the town of Zaleszczyki near the Romanian border. Fred, who insisted on driving his own car, said that he would meet us there.

Increasing chaos terminated all normal life in Lvov as well. German planes had dropped bombs and the resulting fires burned out of control. Dazed and confused residents staggered about while the number of dead and wounded mounted rapidly. In the evening we went back to our vehicles and together with Richard departed from Lvov. Around midnight, while passing through Tarnopol, we saw many people who appeared to be quite flustered. At last we arrived at seven o'clock the following morning at the center of Zaleszczyki. From that town a bridge led across the Dnestr river into neutral Romania. A most attractive view presented itself in this place. It was no surprise to learn that the town was known as a vacation spot. Now, however, due to the outbreak of war, it was nearly deserted. The swelling stream of refugees had not as yet reached this relatively remote area.

We encountered few difficulties in locating a shelter. Janina and Richard, together with their friends, Mrs. Hella Schoenberg and her son, rented a big room in a nice hotel. Good meals were still available at reasonable prices in some restaurants. Eggs, tomatoes, and grapes, for example, could be bought with little money, while heaps of lemons were offered for sale at a nearby market. I noticed that many apricot trees thrived in this area. Several days later these ideal conditions ceased to exist since an increasing stream of refugees arrived in large numbers. Due to this influx most available lodgings became occupied. Foodstore shelves were soon emptied, and prices for various commodities rose quickly. We waited several hours next to the road while hoping that Fred would soon arrive. Every vehicle that appeared in the distance abruptly raised our expectations, but Fred did not come. We assumed that he would not show up, but then a telegram arrived. In it Fred explained that he had taken another road since the one that led directly to Zaleszczyki was now closed. This report originated from the locality of Kuti. Fred succeeded in establishing a telephone connection, and later there came a money order from him to Janina. Unfortunately, our contact was broken but we soon learned that Fred and his family members had already reached the city of Bucharest in Romania.

The accumulation of refugees increased steadily until Romanian government officials arrived at the border. They provided some Christians with entry visas, but no Jew succeeded in getting one. I also applied for temporary asylum in Romania. My effort was rejected even though I had already received an affidavit of support from my daughters, Hedwig and Yolan, who lived in the United States. The crush at the permit issuing office was so great that Polish borderguards had to use rubber truncheons to maintain a semblance of order.

During the morning hours of September 16, a degrading event occurred. Polish warplanes flew past us the entire day with hardly a pause toward Romania where they sought to be interned. Near midday a rumor spread that the bridge was now open to civilian traffic. This regulation served to create a veritable situation comedy. The bridge at Zaleszczyki had never witnessed anything similar to what now transpired. Many vehicles ran out of fuel, and these were pushed across the border. People who carried bundles on their shoulders entered a country where the fury of war had still not penetrated. Many Polish clergymen also appeared to be making a getaway.

It was imperative for us to make instant decisions. I wanted to proceed into Romania, but Janina could not make up her mind. First, she thought about Mietek and then she worried about Fred. Concurrently, we had no information concerning his escape. In view of the existing situation, I also decided to remain on Polish soil. This difficult resolution, which I greatly regretted later on, determined my harsh destiny. I thought of finding a way to reach my dear family members who lived in Budapest, Hungary. If I would have managed to do so, most likely this would eventually have been a sentence of death.

Red Army units, which upon arrival on September 13 received a joyous welcome from local residents, shut down the border crossing. Then the Soviet officers insisted that their sudden appearance be welcomed by elections, and this imbued us refugees with a feeling of security. Janina tried to adjust to the new state of affairs and gained employment, but I failed in doing so. Due to the prevailing situation, I desired a relocation to the city of Lvov and applied at the town hall of Zaleszczyki for a safe-passage document. Even though I considered remaining here with my companions, I was now determined to leave. I roomed in Lvov with an old acquaintance, Professor David Singer, and his family. Since my sleeping accommodation happened to be near a warm kitchen, I quickly regained strength. I maintained a pleasant association with the Singer family while trying to pursue my own business interests.

The Soviet intruders of Zaleszczyki ordered all remaining refugees to leave the area by the end of November. Before then Janina sent a message to me, announcing her early arrival in Lvov. During the appointed day it was hard to find a taxi that would take me to the distant train depot. Even though the weather turned bitter cold, I wanted to get there before the train's arrival, but due to extensive snowdrifts I waited more than an hour. When asked, the stationmaster said that he did not know the present location of this train. It was not until close to midnight that he learned that it was on fire and stood at a distance of 15 kilometers from our location. My determined driver and I got back into the car and drove along the road near the track. My heart started to beat faster when I saw a column of smoke on the horizon. I only hoped that a serious mishap had not occurred. While nearing the stalled train, we stopped and started to walk through the drifting snow to reach it. While drawing closer I noticed that the smoke orginated from the engine boiler. Feeling relieved, I advanced alongside the passenger cars and called for Janina to show herself. While the wind tended to drown out my voice, I felt that my strength was beginning to wane. Finally, I boarded the passenger cars and ran through them until I located Janina and her two sons. They sat inside a compartment while Janina suffered from a migraine headache. I took hold of her suitcase and told the three of them to alight, but then the train slowly began to move. I jumped off and landed in a snowbank, but Janina stayed aboard. As a consequence we reached Lvov separately. I escorted them to the residence of Professor Katz and remained there until they found a place of their own a short distance away. Even so, I visited them often.

The present Soviet authority introduced a precise method of supervision which obligated us to appear every so often at a police station. There they gave us special passes which consisted of two categories. The first one permitted a favored applicant to remain in the local area. The second one was issued to politically unreliable people. We employed considerable efforts to obtain favorable passes but without success. Some people offered to pay large sums of money for counterfeit residency permits. My host, Professor David Singer, offered to provide me with such a document, but I was reluctant to accept it. Fortunately, I decided to do so since none of my acquaintances who opted to remain in Lvov survived the war. Early on we found work in several shops and this enabled us to live well. Jewish refugees as well as native Poles were sent off to the Soviet Union's interior. To avoid this we exercised caution and spent our nights in different hideaways. Providence failed to reveal events that were about to occur in the near future.

The time came when we had to accept a "Paragraph 11" type of pass which obliged us to clear out of Lvov within eight days. Besides, it was forbidden to come closer than 100 kilometers to the German–Soviet Union demarcation line. We then embarked upon daily excursions, at times on foot or train, to find shelter. We found no authority that wished to accept us. All of them were afraid to become involved with us outcasts. This was a tragic and onerous situation which labeled us, due to our racial designation, as unreliable and unwanted.

Some friends told us about Zbaracz, a town located 29 kilometer east of Tarnopol. While seeing what it consisted of we located a decent place of lodging. We returned to Lvov in order to wind up our affairs and on September 1, 1940, came to occupy our new place of residence. The owner of this building, known as Professor Mueller, was 71 years old. Since he could converse in several languages, I regarded him as an erudite scholar. Due to an acute loss of hearing, he liked to retire at an early hour. Even so, Professor Mueller had a remarkable memory, and it was a pleasure to hear him speak. He had a quiet wife who happenened to be a good housekeeper. We considered ourselves to be fortunate to have found this place. The neat house was located close by an intersection of the main thoroughfare, named Street of September 17. No difficulties were encountered when we registered our names at the local municipality. Since the documents were in good order we could now find work again.

Zbaracz sheltered some ten thousand inhabitants. Among these, one third each were Poles, Ukrainians, and Jews. The remains of an old castle stood atop a nearby hill where subterranean passages were later used by threatened Jews as places of refuge. The town's nucleus consisted of a cloister, several churches, synagogues, a high school, and a townhall. Residential buildings appeared to be clustered around this central area.

We left most of our meager possessions with Professor Katz as well as with Dr. Singer in Lvov. Richard then volunteered to help us in retrieving them. I suddenly felt very ill and upon returning home I had to be physically supported. Richard, together with a resident of Zbaracz, who happened to be in Lvov, lent a hand in doing so. Dr. Landau and Dr. Bilinsky came quickly to examine me, but while being taken to the nearby hospital I lost consciousness. The physicians determined that I had sustained an apparently slight foot injury that had turned into a case of blood poisoning. The attending medical men expressed doubt about my recovery, but Janina pulled all levers in an effort to save my life. Since there existed a shortage of medicines in Zbaracz, Janina obtained whatever was needed through the assistance of her son, Mietek. Dr. Landau caused me to feel severe pain while performing surgery on my lymph gland. Thanks to the good care and my strong will to survive, the danger receded gradually. I remained in this hospital for two months until being allowed to go home. I still needed another three months to fully recover. Once again, as so often in my life, I escaped just before the door shut. Perhaps fate wanted to keep me for quite different tests.

Dr. Landau, who treated my illness, was a kind-hearted soul. I recall that during the medical intervention without anesthetics he asked to be forgiven for having caused me so much pain. I also appreciated the good services rendered by Russian nurses. Wearing snow-white coats and felt-lined boots, they radiated an angelic aura.

In the meantime I received several reassuring letters from Christine as well as from my siblings in Budapest. While recovering gradually from my severe illness I began to anticipate better days ahead. Destiny, however, decreed otherwise since it conveyed me as well as my dear ones directly into a previously unimaginable place of purgatory.

[3]

I listened to alarming radio reports on June 22 that informed the native population about Hitler's decision to embark upon a massive invasion of the Soviet Union. I sensed immediately with understandable pleasure that this meant the end of Hitler. Red Army soldiers, quartered here, sought to induct able-bodied men into new military units. This distressing turn of events surprised the local residents even though such a move should have been expected. Soon, a multitude of exhausted people arrived in Zbaracz. During the hot days of summer we provided these thirsty refugees with badly needed water. We filled bottles and containers which they brought along. According to broadcasts the advance of German forces could not be checked. The local population, due to this disastrous report, became confused and helpless. We watched heavily loaded motor vehicles as they raced through dust-clouds toward the east. Several acquaintances who lacked a plan also decided to flee. It may have been prudent for me to join the panicky throng, but I knew that the anticipated hardships could not be endured. I therefore decided to remain where I was.

Early the next day sounds of artillery became audible from the direction of Brody while warplanes appeared overhead to seek out targets. Since we were already used to fleeing from uncontrolable events, this too was taken in stride. Even so, at the very last moment we looked for a vehicle, but our efforts were futile.

Frightened citizens, eager to obtain bread, besieged the local bakery while the noise of artillery kept growing in intensity. Early next morning panicky residents sought to leave town but we, as newcomers, opted to stay out of sight. Since we were associated with few local people, no one wanted to take us along. Under these circumstances we had no choice but to remain here and await whatever was in store. It seemed as if this town had suddenly lost many of its residents. The ones who stayed behind expressed strong feelings of anxiety. Even the local postmaster had already loaded his stocks into a vehicle and disappeared rapidly. We learned that Russian soldiers intended to destroy with explosives the administration building, which happened to be located in our vicinity. This however was not done. Gripped by fear, we brought our meager possessions to the residence of a friend who occupied a room near the marketplace. We now had nothing more than a suitcase and a hatbox which contained our scant material wealth.

Judging from the thunder of approaching gunfire, we realized that the German advance easily penetrated makeshift obstructions and our determined foes would soon be here. Inside our building there now remained only three families besides an old woman who had been abandoned by fleeing relatives. Numerous explosions shook the ground under our feet during July 2, 1941. We beheld large clouds of black smoke and then a sea of bright flames in the distance. Soviet soldiers, who sought to evade an entrapment, proceeded to destroy their remaining supply of petrol. In order to acquaint ourselves with ongoing events, we went out into the street during mid-afternoon. Just then, the enemy launched an artillery barrage which forced us back into our dwelling. The detonations created an ear-splitting noise, and it seemed as if the world was coming to an end. While my eardrums began to throb and ache, the old professor became agitated and with shaking limbs retreated into the cellar. After the departure of all Soviet forces the streets in this town appeared to be depopulated.

Expecting an early appearance of German military vehicles, I stood near the window of our room and observed the main thoroughfare. Janina, Richard, and Mrs. Mueller remained nearby. Indeed, the first hostile armored vehicles covered by Swastika flags advanced slowly and a line of tanks soon followed them. The senile educator, who was nearly deaf and blind, refused to emerge from the cellar. He saw and heard nothing of whatever transpired in the street. More tanks arrived and several projectiles were fired into suspected points of resistance. While gunners observed nearby hills, more shooting occurred, but then there ensued a protracted interval of silence.

Once more we approached the window to gaze upon a scene of confusion. As motor vehicles rolled along the street, it began to rain. Just then, an old woman, who seemed to have lapsed into a state of shock, walked aimlessly along while burning houses illuminated the stark scene. It was hard for us to gain some respite from the hectic activities of soldiers who moved around continually. Some officers ordered us to carry out certain tasks, and we had to comply instantly. Consequently, our stove remained in constant use. Alert soldiers discovered the presence of an egg depot, and soon many eggs were taken from there and we prepared them for the hungry soldiers as though we were on an assembly line. I was astonished to see that some of them devoured up to fifteen eggs in one sitting. We also had to make huge amounts of coffee.

These German infantrymen appeared to be amiable and left us enough to eat. The German soldiers acted generally in a correct manner toward us. How could it happen that these people would be used for such cruel purposes? The invading soldiers, many of whom came from Bavaria and Austria, discovered several barrels filled with beer at the local brewery. Since I was able to speak the Bavarian dialect, they invited me to join them. Momentarily I felt as if I had been magically conveyed back to Munich. These men installed a camp-kitchen near my building and proceeded to slaughter three pigs. They then collected the fat that must have weighed forty kilos. In the meantime a sizeable bivouac arose, and Jewish residents were conscripted as workers. Officers in charge shared some of the food and even permitted the Jewish workers to take home a large quantity of leavings.

The German soldiers informed us about roving formations of SS troops and spoke of their hostile intentions. For us, such admonitions served as a bitter drop in our drinking cups. A nearly continuous stream of German military formations showed up here. These did not stop but moved on in the direction of hitherto unknown regions. Consisting of infantry, artillery, tanks, and motorcycles, these units advanced through our streets at a high rate of speed. The superior condition of this armed host amazed me, and I could not help noticing the well-tailored uniforms worn by officers of higher rank.

Then came July 4, 1941, a date which the local Jewish community designated as "Black Friday." While this formidable war machine advanced swiftly into far-flung regions, a force of malevolent demons was on its way to torment us. This troop arrived with black insignias on their vehicles at a predawn hour. The SS! An indescribable feeling of trepidation constricted my throat and caused me to gasp for air. It was eerie. I momentarily visualized the approach of relentless killers whose vehicles resembled coffins on wheels. Perspiration soon covered my brow while the blue sky seemed to be turning dark.

An extreme state of panic prevailed in the town while SS soldiers dominated the streets. We received an introduction to the unfolding drama early in the morning when the two synagogues were set on fire, and a reign of terror commenced afterwards. Initially, several Jewish dwellings were ransacked, and then one horrendous act of violence followed another in rapid succession. Near my house, for example, there lived a man known as Mr. Hindes who used to trade in cereals. An SS soldier who confronted him insisted on confiscating the keys to his storeroom. Mr. Hindes explained that these had previously been taken away by the Soviet authorities. While the furious SS man reviled him in a vicious manner, two of his comrades were attracted by the scolding. One of them then drew his pistol and shot Mr. Hindes at close range. Having done so, he lit a cigarette and calmly continued his conversation. Mr. Hindes's wife, who was reluctant to go near the body of her husband, came out later and dragged the dead man as far as the fence of her garden. The corpse remained there for many hours. The distraught woman came out several times during the night and lamented near the corpse. The wheat merchant's body was finally removed by two Jewish men with a wagon early in the morning a day later. They buried Mr. Hindes adjacent to the gutted synagogue building. Mrs. Hindes was murdered several days later in a similar manner.

A very pretty young woman, named Gusti Segal, who also resided in Zbaracz, was seized under the pretext of helping to identify someone. The SS men brought her into an empty room where she was severely raped. The daughter of Mr. Goldapfel, a former postal employee, received similar treatment. All of these women were put to death later on. Indeed an appropriate demonstration of the principles of racial purity!

When the South German soldiers withdrew with their field kitchen, they could not take along a nice Telefunken radio. They asked me to accept this radio as their present. Even their captain tried to persuade me and rejected my concerns. These splendid people most likely did not know their own countrymen in the SS. I managed nevertheless to get them to remove the radio which they had already taken to our door. Once again I had predicted the events correctly. One day a SS officer showed up with a man in plain clothes. In rude tones I was accused of having stolen a radio. My response that I did not own a radio and my retelling of the events resulted in their screaming at me, although I said: "You can shoot me if you find a radio in my place." Subsequently I was treated very roughly. They searched the house and everything was turned over. Fortunately, a neighbor was summoned by Janina who had witnessed how I had refused to accept the radio. What would have happened had I accepted the radio as a present? It would have been my end.

These *Razzien* (police raids) were carried out by SS troopers and often lasted many hours. Most of these overzealous soldiers were withdrawn from Zbaracz on July 7. They moved to Tarnopol like a blood-thirsty swarm of locust where larger numbers of potential victims awaited their arrival. There they slaughtered some five thousand Jews within a period of seven days. Max Froehlich, a nephew of Professor Mueller, whose wound was not life-threatening, remained among a pile of corpses.

After having revived adequately, he fled during the night to the home of an acquaintance who summoned a trusted physician to render medical aid. Soon Mr. Froehlich was strong enough to return to Zbaracz where he showed me his wound, located near the stomach.

When the SS soldiers had been suddenly withdrawn from this town, our frayed nerves benefited immensely from a benign interval. Even so, we realized that our chances of escaping from this entrapment now diminished greatly. Currently there was a relative calm after the withdrawal of the SS, and now that the tension of the past days had relented some of the awfulness of our experiences was starting to sink in. It was not until now that we comprehended what the canteen soldiers had meant when they warned us about the SS and when they described their methods to us. But even if we had known everything then, what could we have done? There was no escape for us. It was terrible to see the evil approach, without defense, without a plan, delivered up to certain destruction. That crushes one. But even now my faith in God did not leave me once. It held me up and gave me strength to console my fellow sufferers to enable them to bear everything as I did.

A newly organized group of mercenaries, consisting of Ukrainian militiamen, came to reenforce the remaining SS garrison. Members of this group displayed a strong degree of hostility toward Jews right from the start. They applied various methods of tormenting people on a daily basis. These recruits seemed to derive great satisfaction from the degradation of religious Jews by cutting off their beards. The new authoritarians, who forced Jewish men to perform difficult tasks, now addressed them as "Du Jude," and many other degrading expressions were added as well.

The self-styled German overlords installed a number of functionaries. These included a local commandant, a farm supervisor, and a land commissar. While the chicaneries of the first mentioned one remained tolerable, the remaining two officers behaved themselves in a most hateful and sadistic manner. We feared these brutal men and tried to avoid them as much as possible. The farm supervisor, known as Pfeiffer, always appeared in public carrying a whip. The land commissar called himself Von Braunschweig and deported himself like a king in his domain. Our three tyrants liked to take part in raucous feasts that evolved into veritable orgies. Whenever such revelries took place, we expected boisterous behavior and much shooting throughout the night. At one time, while the revelers were in a mischievous mood, they began to ring the church bells. Fellow drinkers sometimes entered Jewish dwellings to look for women and destroy furnishings. Being unable to voice complaints about these nocturnal activities, we remained helpless.

Janina applied for and received employment at the reopened post office near our house. Then an SS officer showed up and ordered her, together with Mrs. Marie Segal, the sister of Max Froelich, to accompany him. In order to intimidate the woman he escorted them through a number of detours. He finally brought them to a place where they had to wash a stack of soiled military uniforms. While the SS guard walked away from his post, Janina asked a passing woman to inform me about her whereabouts. I then hurried over and got up enough nerve to confront a German soldier who guarded this depot. I asked him: "You certainly also have a wife. What would you do if something like this happened to her?"

This type of approach was effective. It seemed as if the sentry realized that what he did was wrong and he replied by offering me a cigarette which I courteously declined to accept. In this manner I succeeded in gaining the release of both women. Later, Mrs. Segal, her husband, and their two young daughters were arrested and taken to be shot. The fired bullet failed to kill Mrs. Segal instantly. While lying in a prepared trench, she regained consciousness and somehow returned to her house. The SS men wasted little time in recapturing and executing her on the spot.

When the postal services began to function once again, I welcomed this event since it enabled me to resume my correspondence with Christine in Munich. I hoped to receive cheerful reports from her. Besides I wrote a letter addressed to my siblings in Budapest. Even though destiny decreed that we remain separated from each other, we could still take advantage of communicating in this manner. My sisters, Sida and Irma, were born in Vienna, but our parents had taken them to Budapest at an early age. Even so, due to their grandparents' land of origin they were classified as Polish subjects. Many days elapsed until I received a reply from them. It consisted of a postcard, dated August 19, 1941. The message read as follows:

Dear Jenö:

Viktor, Irma, and I have been underway for two weeks since we were compelled to leave home. Here in Borszczow [Poland] we obtained a place of refuge, but we do not know how long it will last. Could you arrange for us to come to Zbaracz? If this card reaches you please reply at once.

Many kisses, your Sida.

Viktor Blum, Irma's fiancee, had also been expelled together with thousands of others from Hungary. My reply to Sida could hardly he consoling. In the meantime most dismal placards appeared in our streets. These proclaimed the following message: "The departure of Jews from this district is strictly forbidden. The penalty for disobeying this order is death!"

August 31, 1941

With great joy we received your cards of August 26 and 28. The knowledge that you are healthy in Zbaracz is a ray of sun between the black clouds. We wish for a reunion soon with you. We endured very difficult days.

September 6, 1941

Viktor is doing all he can to conserve his strength. Even though he is getting weaker from day to day we are holding on. Our future prospects appear to be very bleak since we lack financial resources. The authorities allowed us to take along no more than a filled rucksack. We are constantly thinking about what to do next but cannot find an answer. Please let us know if you can help us.

Unfortunately I was hardly in a position to render aid since my own status happened to be one of desperation.

September 14, 1941

There are often days when we have to suffer tremendously. In our dreams we cry and wake each other. Our pillows are then wet from tears.

September 15, 1941

In response to your questions I must tell you that everything happened too fast. First Irma became ill with excitement and was taken to the hospital. After four days, I had to leave our lovely home, the fruit of my life. I met Irma again on a train after a long search. We had a very sad trip. We finally arrived after eight hours here in Borszczow. We all had to walk a lot. There is no work whatsoever.

September 16, 1941

I can assure you we are not suffering since Viktor is trying everything to make our current, hopefully temporary, existence easier for us. We have gotten used to being here and Viktor even wanted to make life easier for you. We received your money. We will get everything right again.

September 29, 1941

We received your cards of the 20th and 22nd along with the money transfers. Thank you for everything. We could do a lot with this money. We also thank you for your good wishes. I cried a lot and thought of the times when we were all together.

October 6, 1941

Without waiting for your mail I am sending off a few lines. We always think what would be best, this way or that. But we cannot find a way out. If we only had a job, then our minds and souls would be busy. Do not forget the anniversary of our dear father's death on October 14th!

October 10, 1941

I keep trying to write to our brothers in Budapest. I do not know why no mail reaches Budapest from here, yours always gets here.

October 17, 1941

I thank you for your birthday wishes and I would be glad if we could be together soon.

October 18, 1941

It seems that we will have to change our place of residence and return to the one we occupied last year. Worsening weather conditions are causing a great deal of suffering. I wish that God would grant us peace.

Sida

These messages disclosed the fact that my dear sister endured days of frustration and suffering. Even though she did not dare to elaborate, I recognized their difficult situation by reading between the lines. Especially the remarks about the weather indicated a worsening situation. They still hoped for an opportunity to return home. A letter, originating from my brother. Lajos in Budapest arrived later. He informed me about the following:

October 16, 1941

I wish to let you know that I submitted an application to the government to permit Irma and Sida to return to Hungary and received an official confirmation in this matter. We still remain hopeful.

Lajos

Our harrowing existence continued while various methods to make our cheerless lives more miserable were implemented. I doubted that our degrading position would decline further, but it did become much, much worse. One day our oppressors posted new orders. These stated: "All German soldiers must be greeted by the local inhabitants at all times!" Later on, the tyrants rescinded this demand and instructed us not to greet them. Many German soldiers also became confused and remained unsure about what was proper. If a military vehicle passed by and Jewish pedestrians failed to greet its occupants, the offenders received a thrashing. Unfortunately, the hapless people were treated similarly if they did greet them. Whenever we could not decide quickly enough how to comply, our most expedient response consisted of hiding ourselves. The Germans decided to display placards that showed an oversized louse on the walls of buildings. A caption instructed the public: "Take care. Jews carry disease-spreading vermin. Be vigilant while approaching Jews!"

Hardly a day passed without various kinds of unpleasant incidents. Once I was forced to join a work team consisting of nearly one hundred men and women. In accordance with our assignment we toiled at repairing railroad tracks while being guarded by Ukrainian militiamen. Under these harsh circumstances we felt like condemned felons.

On September 6, 1941, it was announced that Jewish men between the ages of sixteen and sixty were to gather at the local marketplace at seven o'clock in the morning. Wanting to be there on time I arose well before daybreak. In order to create a favorable impression, I prepared myself with extra care. When I was ready to leave my dwelling, I noticed that the exit door had been locked. I demanded that Janina give me the key, but she steadfastly refused to do so. She had a premonition that nothing but an ill-fated event was bound to occur there. I surrendered willingly to her sixth sense and then approached the window. From that vantage point I observed the men as they proceeded toward the marketplace.

Initially, due to my absence, I expected an ugly confrontation but several minutes after seven there arose a sudden panic at the square. The crowd became frightened and dispersed in every direction. Then, SS soldiers, assisted by Ukrainian auxiliaries, quickly surrounded the entire area and attacked the frightened people with truncheons. After having subdued them, they determined the ages and occupations of the captives. Then they divided the people into two separate divisions. The first one included those who appeared to belong to the local intelligentsia. The second group consisted of all the others. The Germans assembled the latter batch in rows of four and it was taken out to perform laborious tasks. The first group, consisting of 72 men, was detained as hostages.

Besides, the Germans imposed a specific task to be carried out within a specified limit of time. Items to be delivered by noon included five kilograms of tea, five kilograms of coffee, 150 kilograms of sugar and 200 bars of soap. In order to gain an early release of their men, the women gathered the required items as quickly as possible. They dashed from one house to the next in an effort to fill the quota. Everything had been collected in time but, contrary to expectations, the hostages were not released. Instead, the Germans loaded them onto trucks that departed toward a secret destination. While underway, the hapless men had to remain in a kneeling position with lowered heads. Later on, peasants told of having heard much shooting and then coming across fresh burial sites. They also found discarded documents in the area. From that time on devised maltreatments increased in volume until they were odious.

The authorities then demanded the creation of a *Judenrat* (Council of Jews). The main task of this body consisted not of aiding people but of delivering them to the butchers. A Pinkus Gruenfeld was selected to play a most sinister role in the unfolding drama when he attained the rank of chairman of this nefarious council. Several other ambitious men sought to gain advantages as well by assembling victims. Eventually, these collaborators also came to a sad end. So as to enforce its resolve, the Judenrat organized a Jewish militia unit. Younger men who wished to advance their own status decided to join this special body. Ultimately, however, our council chairman opted to abuse them by implementing harmful schemes.

Initially, the militia members were few in numbers, but with the passage of time their membership increased rapidly. One adherent of this force, named Winitzky, proved to be a most egotistical man, and for this reason Gruenfeld assigned him to engage in unpleasant tasks. Every Jew in town wished to avoid nasty encounters with this person.

The Judenrat office demanded a financial contribution and my share was 500 zlotys. Militiamen, who functioned as bailiffs, carried out this collection in a meticulous manner. Poor people, who could not come up with reasonable amounts of cash, were deprived of objects that appeared to be of equal value. Various sorts of utensils such as cupboards, beds, linen, pots and pans were confiscated. Our Judenrat also established an *Arbeitsamt* (labor office) where corruption reigned supreme. So-called permanent positions could be attained only for large sums of money.

Those who were fortunate enough to acquire such jobs often benefited from a long-term postponement of being sent to an extermination camp. Some desperate souls paid up to 3,000 zlotys to obtain road construction assignments and even larger sums for employment at the eastern railroad. Dr. F. held a rather humble position as a translator, but still he played a prominent role. Later on he was advanced to the weighty assignment of hiring laborers. The Judenrat sought to compete with the enterprise of Dr. F. by recruiting toilers. Concurrently, the Tarnopol branch of the German construction firm Heckmann announced that it needed skilled workers. Mietek, who was accepted for employment by this company, then relocated together with others to Tarnopol. However, Professor Mueller's daughter as well as her husband and their eight-year-old son stayed with us. These people hoped to find decent jobs and a more benign lifestyle.

Meanwhile, the dire condition of my sister Sida, who could not leave Borszczow, worsened steadily. This knowledge had a paralyzing effect on me while I sought, according to my limited ability, to render aid. She then sent a letter that contained the following message:

October 24, 1941

Dear Jenö:

I hereby confirm having received your card together with the money transfer of October 20. Do not send me more money since you need it yourself. I assume that you got my message concerning our enforced detention here. Letters to Budapest are not accepted by our postoffice.

We are constantly worrying about our dear ones.

November 4, 1941

We received your card of October 31 and cried with joy that you have the news from our brothers Miksa and Lajos that they are doing well and that they are both working. A heavy load has been taken off our shoulders.

Unprecedented events occurred in Zbaracz with increasing frequency, Placards that were posted on walls of houses informed us that an exchange of old Polish banknotes would soon take place. This notice explained that equal amounts in new issues would now start to circulate. I took my remaining 440 zlotys to the Ukrainian bank, and it provided me with a receipt. Later, it sent me a notice in reference to this transaction. It brought to my attention the fact that I would receive the stipulated amount only if I furnished the bank with proof of Aryan ancestry. Obviously I was unable to do so.

A newly issued order declared: "Jews are hereby obligated to give up their fur and woolen garments!" Soon another debasing demand arrived: "All Jews from the age of fourteen may appear in public only when wearing a ten-centimeter-wide armband showing a blue Star of David on the right arm. Noncompliance with the order will result in severe punishments!" Two days later our captors demanded that all armbands had to be displayed on the left, instead of the right arm. Two days later this order was rescinded: on the right arm! This rule was strictly enforced and the penalty for disobedience consisted of a payment amounting to 500 zlotys. Later, members of our community faced a penalty of death. Additional notices informed us that not only Jews were obligated to obey this rule but also those who claimed to be Christians but could not furnish proof of Aryan ancestry.

The local command post and the district commissar needed curtains, office furniture, and kitchen implements. In order to acquire these items, the venal Mr. Gruenfeld, accompanied by militiamen, entered Jewish homes and took whatever seemed to be of value. They loaded everything onto wagons and left us even more destitute than before.

Soon another, different type of directive plagued us. This one dealt with a display of posters, embellished with a Star of David, on our doors and windows. The callous despots were not satisfied with various designs and demanded uniform ones. The new placards were adorned with three official signatures. These posters were sold to helpless Jewish residents for a payment of 100 zlotys each. The local authority cautioned the native peasantry not to enter homes that displayed these emblems.

Daily existence for the Jewish population became ever more burdensome. Even though most able-bodied men were occupied by various laborious tasks, they received few compensations. In spite of the fact that most Jews never had enough money, the Judenrat demanded steady contributions. Residents who managed to retain something helped in alleviating the hunger of destitute neighbors. Due to this predicament, ever more people became dependent upon the Judenrat for assistance. Later on, they paid for this dependence with their lives.

According to a previous notification, Jews were forbidden to dispose of their possessions since these had been foreclosed by the authority. In spite of such prohibitions, residents sold articles of clothing in secret. They gave some of their last remaining shirts to local peasants in exchange for food. Trying to avoid illness due to malnutrition, they engaged in risky transactions. The native peasants had few scruples about exploiting hungry Jews. Stiff punishments were imposed upon those who were caught, but the most severe chastisements were inflicted upon the intimidated Jewish inhabitants. Such offenders were obliged to report to a Ukrainian militia post where they encountered rough receptions and contracts were made out on mere scraps of paper. Sometimes the Ukrainian officers threatened to forward dubious documents to the German Security Service (SD) office in Tarnopol.[2]

The local detainees knew full well that such a move would result in a sentence of death. Therefore, Ukrainian militiamen proceeded on their own accord. Besides cash, they freely accepted various items of value such as rings, clothes, and valises. So as to facilitate these procurements the Judenrat employed middlemen who performed special tasks. These consisted of instructing ghetto leaders to confiscate various useful objects from people who existed under their supervision. The Ukrainian puppet then destroyed incriminating documents if the items he received turned out to be useful. Ukrainian peasants also employed able-bodied Jews as farm laborers and they were allowed to take home portions of confiscated foods. This practice enabled us to buy meat, eggs, and flour from them. Every Jew feared to enter the open market since agricultural inspectors were often present. Besides, Nazi agents were constantly on the lookout for the appearance of unwanted non-Aryans.

Ghetto inmates received orders to maintain clean sidewalks next to their houses. Whoever failed to do so was threatened with punishment. The aggressive Ukrainian militia took advantage of its limited authority by forwarding unfavorable reports to the Germans as a lucrative source of income. Whenever an efficient inspector resolved to apply his authority to forward unfavorable reports concerning Jewish habitations he could easily find specks of dirt. The penalty for an offense such as this ranged from 25 to 50 zlotys, depending on the examiner's mood. He recorded the arbitrary transaction on an ordinary piece of paper. Since Jews had already been classified as outlaws, none of them dared to protest these senseless procedures.

The oddyssey encountered by my sisters, Sida and Irma, was inevitably terminated. The postcard I received from them on November 9, was their last sign of life.

I confirm your card of November 2. Calm yourself, we acquired heating material during these days. Hopefully it will last for four to five weeks. For this we traded our last items because we are well taken care of when we have a warm place. Currently we have no further plans than the expectation that our days will soon improve.

The cards I sent out after this date remained unanswered. The postoffice in Borszczow returned my cards on November 22, 1941, with the remark: "Addressee Deceased!"

While struggling to obtain the most basic food supply for our survival, I now suffered from emotional pain. I implored my Judenrat office to initiate an inquiry and it verified the fact that a pogrom had taken place in Borzczow. The slaughter was carried out by SS soldiers on November 14 in response to a strong speech delivered on November 9, by Josef Goebbels, the Nazi propaganda minister.

It was difficult for me to cope with this awful tragedy but shortly thereafter I received a message from the Red Cross organization in Budapest. It informed me that Sida had left Budapest in an effort to find me. In desperation I communicated with the Judenrat of Borszczow and it sent me the following reply:

THE COUNCIL OF JEWS
IN BORSZCZOW
On December 9, 1941
Number 307/41

To
J. Littner
in Zbaraz

In reply to your letter of Dec. 5, 1941 we inform you that Sida Littner, Irma Littner and Viktor Blum died on November 14, 1941 in Boszczow and were buried on this day at the Jewish cemetery of this place.

For the Council of Jews

[illegible signature]

I will never find the grave of my beloved ones. No Jew will have survived the massacres of Borszczow. Even though I did not have much hope, I did not give up inquiring about their fate. How much they suffered, how they must have patiently carried their destiny in the foolish hope for better times, until suddenly a cold and brutal will extinguished the defenseless souls. What a heroic deed it must be to kill defenseless human beings with heavy weaponry! Their poor souls accuse us but they remind mankind at the same time to respect the highest human dignity and to honor the life of others and to leave death to God.

ABSENDER

DER JUDENRAT
in BORSZCZOW

Distr. Galizien

II.41.

POSTKARTE

12

GENERAL GOUVERNEMENT

BO... 12.(... (DISTR GALIZIEN)

An

J. Littner

bei Müller

Zbaraz

Konovalecgasse 25

Distr. Galizien

DER JUDENRAT
in BORSZCZOW
am 9. December 1941.
Zahl 307/41.

An
J. Littner
in Zbaraz

In Beantwortung Ihres Schreibens vom 5. XII. 1941 teilen wir mit, dass Littner Sida, Littner Jrna und Blum Wiktor am 14. November 1941 in Borszczów gestorben sind und an diesem Tag auf dem hiesigen jüdischen Friedhofe bestattet worden sind. —

Für den Judenrat:

Sekretär

Near the end of 1941 a gang of Nazis with violent intentions entered our residence at four o'clock in the morning. While the six of us were still asleep, our door was opened with great force. Three heavily armed SD soldiers stormed in. They immediately belabored us with rubber truncheons and then herded us into a corner. I actually expected to be beaten to death. The intruders inflicted numerous welts on our heads and bodies. The deaf and senile Mr. Mueller was not spared either. He whimpered like a hurt child when one of the brutes knocked the eyeglasses off his face. I still had enough boldness to exclaim: "Be considerate of this old man; he is deaf!"

My urgent pleas were simply ignored. After the wreckers ransacked all that was useable, they entered the kitchen but found few objects that interested them. They merely took two eggs and then smashed them on the floor. They also scattered salt, flour, and a small quantity of ersatz coffee. After having completed this vile exploit, the ruthless marauders decided to leave us in peace and then moved on to another dwelling. There, they broke windowpanes and confiscated clothes, shoes, and provisions. Peasants, eager to gain benefits from this bizarre situation, stood by with their carts. The mayor of Zbaracz, Mr. Toporowitz, also appeared to witness ongoing events, but he failed to berate the looters. This hurtful activity did not abate until ten o'clock in the morning. It was planned by a so-called *Strafkommando* (punishment squad) which derived from SD headquarters in Tarnopol.

A certain branch of the Tarnopol job procurement office established itself in our town on January 30, 1942. It provided Jewish men between the ages of 14 and 60 with identity cards and passport pictures. Everyone in this category was obliged to report to the labor bureau once every week. The main purpose of this measure was to distribute the more able-bodied Jewish men to various labor camps. Genuine work assignments, except those at road construction and laboring at the eastern railroad track, were few in number. Private firms lacked the right to employ Jews. Since nearly every labor camp had its own cemetery, we already knew what transpired there. The director of our local labor procurement office, a Mr. Wasuta, still nurtured basic human feelings even though he was a strict man. In contrast, we regarded his secretary, a Mr. Siwy, as a fear-inspiring creature. Those who reported to him were bound to get unpleasant assignments as inmates of forced labor camps.

The number of men who showed up decreased rapidly. Many of them were being sent to *Straflager* (punishment camps) where they had to perform hard labor. Then, mostly older people and children remained in Zbaracz. The labor procurement secretary, Mr. Siwy, wished to send me to the Straflager in Maximova but Mr. Wasuta, the director, intervened in my behalf. He provided me with a local assignment. In time Mr. Wasuta absconded from the clutches of his Nazi masters and never returned. I realized that this man disagreed with the brutal Nazi tactics. He even provided some women with Aryan papers and this enabled them to go to Germany.

Fortunately, I obtained the good position of supervising a team of sanitation workers. My main responsibility consisted of maintaining cleanness in the streets. The crew consisted mainly of senile men whose performance proved to be inadequate. I therefore advised most of them to stay at home, and I performed the required tasks practically by myself. In order to function well I consumed my meager breakfast before dawn and then went out to sweep the streets. Thereby I became my own supervisor. I also urged my neighbors to clean the street in front of their houses. In this manner I sustained myself in this lowly position without incentives, but I was allowed to remain alive.

The employment office assigned me to carry out simple tasks and provided able-bodied men with jobs. This included rendering aid to healthy native residents in accepting work assignments in Germany. There evolved much confusion during the duration of this drive, and it enabled me to become familiar with these so-called volunteers. German securitymen, assisted by the Ukrainian militia, applied coercive methods for ensnaring candidates. Many people were caught during nocturnal hours, and they agreed to comply after an application of force. Some conscripts, while trying to evade pursuers, even sought hiding places in Jewish abodes.

German officialdom granted us no respite in executing their wishes. One ordinance insisted that every adult Jews acquire a standard-sized snapshot. In order to accomplish this, a team of cameramen came all the way from Warsaw, and they remained in this area for an entire week. Each person had to pay a fee of three zlotys for a set of three pictures which none of us ever received.

No messages from my dear son, Zoltan, ever arrived here since our last and final meeting in Krakow. I tried to locate his present whereabouts until I learned that apparently he and his wife were staying in the Warsaw ghetto. I then addressed a letter to the Judenrat office in that city and soon received a reply. It verified the fact that they were actually located in that overcrowded place. My ill-fated son and his wife, Rosalia, then informed me about suffering from extreme hardships while being trapped within this congested ghetto enclave.

Zoltan informed me about the many corpses whose faces were covered with newspapers. I now learned about the awful entrapment of my only son and his good wife, but there was no way for me to intercede on their behalf. Overcome by anger and fear I brought Zoltan's letter to the Judenrat office and begged for an immediate attempt to render aid. The members of this equally helpless body promised to investigate the situation, but there was nothing else they could do. Apparently, Zoltan's letter remained inside a drawer since it was never returned to me. Soon another letter from the Warsaw ghetto reached me and it was dated May 7, 1942:

Warsaw, May 7, 1942

My dear father:

Today I received your letter, a card, and a remittance of money altogether for which I sincerely thank you. Dear father, you cannot possibly imagine in what a situation we were in when we received your letter. Upon my word of honor we had absolutely nothing to eat for the past three days. We already imagined that we would soon die from starvation. Dear father, it is difficult for me to speak of these events but unfortunately, there is really no other way out. Many days passed while I waited for your reply. Dear father, I beg you once more, try to rescue us from here. You state on this card that you think a parcel would help us. In reply I must say that it makes a difference from night to day. I am enumerating several local prices here. The most common bread, made from bran and potato peelings, costs 16 zlotys per kilo. One kilo flour costs 35 zl. One kilo pork lard is 170 zl. One kilo butter is 150 zl. Barley groats cost from 20 to 33 zl. Dear father, can you imagine how a poor man could live here? Actually, we are entirely dehydrated since our mouths had not tasted fat for almost a year. Potatoes cost 6 zl. per kilo. A person is unable to buy the most essential items. I beg you once again, my dear father, if you are able to get us out of here we will absolutely not be a burden to you. My wife and I are used to doing all work no matter how hard it is. Believe me, when I pass by a storewindow I would very much like to smash it in order to take out the bread. If you could see me I would spare myself from writing to you. I am entirely unable to walk up the steps. Dear father, concerning the severe blow you encountered with your dear sisters, I express my sorrow to you with a whole heart and really feel most deeply about the severe misfortune.

The worst for us is that we have no place to live. We drag ourselves from one place to the next and find in addition to our hunger never any rest. I greet and kiss you.

Your ever loyal son, Zoli

Please answer immediately!

Rosalia adds the following:

> Dear father I beg you too. Help us out from this misfortune however it is possible for you. We are in a condition of the greatest danger of life.

1,000 kisses Rosalia

May 10, 1942

My dear good father!

I am writing to you an additional letter. Have just learned that groups which are constantly going to Tarnopol take people from Warsaw to there. Perhaps you can inquire there in what manner. They are coming here with cows. This night horrible things have taken place in the Warsaw ghetto. I do not even want to write you about this. There are here in the Warsaw ghetto some 500,000 Jews, and now several thousand more were brought from Germany and Czechoslovakia. There are 400 to 450 burials each day. The dead are lying three to four weeks in the cemetery. Dear father, I beg you again truly with our last remaining strength, save us in any way you are able to save us. I shall be thankful to you for my entire life. My wife and I will do the hardest work for you and also for ourselves.

Do you hear something from Miksa and Lajos? Dear father, do not be angry with me when I ask for too much from you, but still when I write to you so much of what we experience here cannot be described. Dear father, I will be eternally thankful to you. Dear father, my wife always says if we could stay alive and be with you she would want to wash your feet and to serve you better than her own father. From Lilly and Hedwig I have also received mail during the war. Both of them are well married, Hedwig has borne a child. I am very angry with both because so many people here receive parcels and large valuable ones but from my sisters I had absolutely no help at all. People have lard and tea, and also received various sorts of canned food. How useful this would be for us. My mother always sent us a parcel of 1/2 kg or 1 kg. Today this is also forbidden.

Dear father, I therefore implore you once again, save us and help us. We will be eternally thankful. Only you can save us from death. Therefore save us! I beg you once more for forgiveness since we demand so much, but death stands in front of our eyes.

1,000 kisses your Zoli

After these letters it was no wonder that I was in terrible despair. I found no rest and ran from one acquaintance to another. But nobody knew what to do. I had to watch events unfold; it wore me down. I could eat only with grief. My modest sleeping quarters became painful when I thought of Zoltan. I will not deny the bitter tears of powerless pain during these days. Where in the world would there have been a father with different feelings?

At the post office I tried to call the Judenrat in Warsaw. But it was impossible. Everywhere the death sentence was decreed for leaving the city. The only help were my money transfers to Zoltan. Subsequently, a telegraphed plea for help from my daughter-in-law arrived, followed by a letter:

Warsaw, August 13, 1942

My dear father:

Zoli is unfortunately unable to write himself. Therefore I am writing. Zoli is too weak. He really went through very difficult days and weeks. He had nights with 150 bowel movements and with blood. Doctors and people wonder how he was really able to hold out in such a crisis. Besides, he is swollen everywhere on his entire body where only bones exist. Doctors say that all this came only from hunger. Unfortunately, I suffer from the same illness, however, I must thank God for not being in the same condition as poor Zoli. When I sent the telegram, Zoli had a fever of 41.8 degrees. He was in such a condition that I believed he would die before the telegram would reach you. Doctors admired Zoli still today since he had such severe complications. For example, out of 152 cases one person from among these would still be alive. That is death for 99 percent. Zoli had to sleep in hallways for four weeks since no one wanted to let him come into their dwellings. If I want to do what the doctor requests with injections and artificial nourishment, this would cost us 150 zlotys. He also advised drinking 3 liters of cow's milk per day. The liter costs 15 zlotys. I do not want to write to you anymore since it would only create a heavy heart for the dear father. If at least I would be in good health, but I am also too weak to write this letter. It costs me my final strength. Therefore you must also not be angry about not receiving a message from us for such a long time. We received your 100 zlotys but we already owed the entire amount. Dear father, you are our sole salvation so that Zoli, when his condition improves, will be able to stand and walk again. In the meantime there exists no chance for an improvement of his health. In reality, we are lost like two birds during a severe winter frost. If your Judenrat would establish a contact with the one in Warsaw in regard to this matter this must surely be achieveable. If I had the needed amount of money we could have joined you a long time ago. I would have had a chance for getting a pass. Dear father, please do not let us die here but continue to help us in any way you can. Greetings to Korngold and 1,000 kisses.

                                                    Rosalia and the unlucky Zoli

That was the last news from the famine-hell of Warsaw. My subsequent communications as well as money transfers went unanswered. Soon thereafter it was decided to terminate all postal services for Jews. The whole world knows what happened in the Warsaw ghetto. I never heard from Zoltan or Rosalia again. Also this star in my journey through the night was extinguished. Fate had finished one of the most touching chapters in the book of my suffering. But it hurried to begin the chapter that followed. At this time I also received more sad news from Munich. Christine reported the death of her mother. Her pain was also mine.

Reports from Lvov indicated that an intensification of violence was in the offing. Mr. Singer who worked at the Judenrat office told me that there existed no hope for an improvement of our precarious situation. On the contrary, it was bound to worsen. The dreaded SS *Himmelfahrtskommando* (SS Ascension Day Command) now started to accelerate its diabolic activities. This fanatical association of anti-Semites demanded a speedy surrender of many Jews in order to terminate their earthly existence. Some ghetto representatives bravely refused to comply with this order. They themselves paid a supreme price for this show of obstinacy. The Jews in Warsaw, driven by sheer desperation, opted to fight well-armed SS units.

In accordance with Hitler's order to extirpate the so-called inferior Jewish race, the maltreatment of Jews increased in ferocity. The mere sight of a Jew in our streets provoked the Germans to react violently. So as to breathe fresh air while staying out of sight, depending on the weather, we remained at the back of our houses. While suffering from moods of desperation, we wished to keep the glowing days of summer from vanishing.

The date was August 30, 1942. Since we encountered no opportunity to avoid this predicament, we felt quite despondent. While visiting neighbors, our conversation concerned itself primarily with unpleasant current events. Before falling asleep frightening thoughts of doom tormented my brain. The brother of Professor Halpern, who lived in our house, attained the high position of vice-chairman at our Judenrat headquarter. It happened that two Jewish policemen visited us late in the evening and brought an urgent message from Professor Halpern. The latter felt overwhelmed by urgent official tasks, and he needed assistance in the office. Since this summons from the Judenrat served as a warning of imminent danger, we got dressed at once.

An hour later someone knocked on our door. We felt nervous and fearful while complying with this warning signal and left our house through a rear door. Surrounded by darkness we went down an embankment and suddenly there appeared two Jewish policemen who directed the beam of a flashlight into our faces. They assumed that we wanted to flee and cautioned us not to provoke a dangerous confrontation with the authorities. Later on we learned that the person who knocked on our door was sent by Professor Halpern in order to inform us about the start of an *Aktion* (stalking of Jews). Even though we expected an occurence of distressing events the message of doom caused us to feel forlorn. We noticed through a window the outlines of soldiers in the nocturnal darkness. They were SS men, looking like ghosts in their white coats, who wanted to get their human prey, a contingent of Jews, to be sent to the Belzec extermination camp. The occupants of this building consisted of Mr. Jakob Oehl, his daughter-in-law, and his four-year-old granddaughter, Noemi. The families Kornberg and Froehlich were also present. A team of elite soldiers entered the vestibule of our house, and then the names of several persons were called out. Included in this list was Jakob Oehl and Mr. and Mrs. Kornberg.

During this time of extreme tension I felt weak in my legs but managed to recover quickly. Even so, after having been spared being summoned to the Final Judgement, I was emotionally drained. Presently, the messengers of doom had gathered no more than three candidates in our house. They escorted the ill-fated ones, who knew that pleading for mercy would fall on deaf ears, to an early demise. I witnessed heartrending scenes near our housedoor, and the ones who were left behind lamented loudly. Due to this emotional upheaval the ensuing commotion in the streets created a spectral scene. Dazed people were taken out from all Jewish houses, and old Mr. Kazu and his wife were among them. Afterwards, someone told me that while being led away he told his spouse in Viennese dialect: "Come along, old one, let us go on a honeymoon!"

The German elite soldiers also wished to arrest Mr. Shapu who lived in our house, but they could not find him. This man had sufficient foresight to prepare for himself a hideaway in the cellar, and presently he could not be found. In expectation of additional dreadful events, we spent the remainder of that night in a state of great apprehension. This event, however, was merely a temporary respite. When Professor Halpern returned to us in the morning, it was hard to look upon his fear-stricken face. Sobbing, he described the repugnant scene inside the Judenrat office.

Gruenfeld had to compile a list, since the SS demanded an immediate delivery of 530 people. The candidates were ejected from their beds, and if anyone whose name appeared on the list could not be found, another resident had to take his place. The stipulated quota, based upon the total number of available Jews, had to be tallied in a precise manner.

The selected death candidates had been confined in the public bathhouse, and the next morning they were loaded onto trucks. Three people who could not climb aboard by themselves were shot without compunction. The well-guarded vehicles then proceeded in the direction of Tarnopol. Young Mr. Oehl, who labored at the railroad track leading into that town, was unaware of the fact that his father had been arrested. While noticing the passing trucks, he saw him standing in one of them. He was forbidden to approach the road nor make attempts to communicate with him. They could only say farewell by gazing upon each other from a distance. Mr. Oehl Sr., who happened to be a friendly and decent man, had now left us and would never return. His little granddaughter, Noemi, had provided him with much delight in his old age. They spent many happy hours together but all of this was now terminated.

During that time we learned that a large killing facility had been built near the town of Belzec and people from our district were scheduled to go there. Soon after the initial Aktion ended in Zbaracz, another drive for financial contributions was launched. The Judenrat chairman established a committee for supervising this effort, however he did not bother to find out if the remaining Jews still had items of value in their possession. I soon discovered that certain members of this nefarious Judenrat contributed nothing. In an effort to while away the long evening hours, these deputies played cardgames for high stakes while consuming ample quantities of alcohol. They also entertained the Jewish militia whose task it was to arrest victims, including their own relatives. The Judenrat delivered every selected victim, including near relatives. It also supplied the Ukrainian milita with candidates for death. Before carrying out such unpleasant tasks, the Jewish militiamen consumed enough spirits to deaden the senses. Ghetto dwellers, hoping to slow down the deportations, surrendered whatever had potential value. We learned that it was possible to curtail additional banishments in this manner.

The time arrived when the occupation authority included every habitation within the district of Tarnopol in the process of becoming *Judenfrei* (free of Jews). More people arrived in our town. These tired-looking newcomers, who carried few possessions, soon found adequate resting places. All men who appeared to have enough strength were singled out and detained in the Judenrat's building courtyard.

All those selected to perform heavy labor were divided into smaller groups to facilitate their shipment to various laborcamps. Some of these installations, supervised by SS soldiers, were referred to as *Schreckenslager* (horror camps). Most of these maintained their own burial sites. Overseers, assigned to work in such institutions, tended quickly to acquire strong sadistic inclinations. One report mentioned a malicious foreman named Ostrovsky. He once attacked a Jewish inmate with a shovel until the latter collapsed in agony. This vicious sadist then emptied his bladder on the dying man's mouth. As soon as the Judenrat in Zbaracz heard about this despicable event, its chairman sent a complaint to the German Security Service. This powerful bureau responded by sending a commission of inquiry, and it recommended that Ostrovsky be transferred to another, distant location.

Hideous events took place in other labor camps. Reports about most inadequate food rations emanated from various places. The Germans introduced a renewed drive for contributions, and these included bread, barley, flour, and lentils. Various other items weighing up to 10 kilos needed to be delivered. We tried hard to comply with these demands according to our capabilities. The Judenrat prepared a number of basic items every Tuesday and Friday for transfer to the Tarnopol labor camps. The price for each contribution ranged from three to five zlotys.

A report that derived from Tarnopol informed us about an Aktion that was carried out in that town, and it claimed many victims. While aware of the fact that Janina's son Mietek resided there in an urban labor camp, we worried about his welfare.[3] It happened that a courier from Tarnopol came to our Judenrat and brought a letter addressed to Janina from Mietek. It contained the following message:

Dear Mother:

The letter you wrote arrived here at last. I cannot describe how happy I was to receive it. Here, near the train station I saw a transport from Zbaracz and I was afraid to see you there. Fortunately you were not among the captives. Feeling relieved I decided to give away my old Russian stamp collection to Gruenfeld. I told him that members of his Judenrat could certainly make use of it. Frightening events have taken place here. Two-thirds of our people in Tarnopol had already been taken away. That is 5,800 out of 9,000 inhabitants. I felt as if the hair stood up on my head when I heard about this. Previously, we were allowed to stay overnight in private rooms here, but on Sunday we received orders to sleep inside the camp. On Monday morning we learned that an Aktion had already started. I could hardly sleep since fleas tormented me continually during the night. One cannot easily forget such an experience. While being plagued by fatigue and nearing a state of collapse, we had to labor with the threshing machine the following day.

I would not wish it upon anyone to witness events that occurred here on bloody Monday. Here and there children, women, and older men, among heartrending screams, were marched off by the Jewish militia, all to the slaughter. I saw desperate people who tried to flee. These were pursued by militiamen and SS soldiers who shot them down. We formed columns while the Jewish leaders, Fink and Wolkenberg, led us from the camp. Looking pale and shaking with fear, we could hardly be recognized. They led us to a place where many people waited for a transport to the Belzec death camp. Initially, we found ourselves among the condemned ones, but fortunately they were allowed to escort us to a worksite. Since I did not wish to return to Tarnopol before the conclusion of this Aktion, I was glad to have the bread you sent me. When the day neared its end, we stopped working and went to the train station where other workers awaited our arrival. We had no idea what to do next. Should we go back to the camp and spend the night there? People who paused near the ghetto entrance advised us not to go in. We accepted their advice and went back to our worksite. We stayed there until morning. I do not know if it was luck when an overseer came to inspect this area since he evicted us from our hiding place. When we entered the ghetto it was already dark. The entrance was unguarded and remained open. It seemed as if a violent furor of war had passed through here. Every house appeared to be empty and windows were broken while corpses littered the streets. This district of Tarnopol was now as silent as a grave. A militiaman approached us and said: "Twelve more people have to be seized in order to conclude this Aktion." We felt a sensation of panic while being confronted by these men but I told them: "We came here as workers from Camp Zbaracz." Thereupon they left us in peace. It seemed a miracle. We were all alone in this depopulated ghetto. Later, another group of workers joined us but a third one decided to retreat into the forest.

Soon, the ongoing manhunt neared its end. Many housedoors were open but no one among us thought of stealing. The Koerner family from Krakow survived. My landlady also had luck since her presence was overlooked, but her 35-year-old daughter was taken away. A former colleague of mine received information about the arrest of her mother. Intent on retrieving her, she deserted her assigned workplace and was taken along as well. Could you possibly send a telegram to my uncle to let him know that we are still alive, even though I am badly in need of bread and sugar. I am sending you some of my laundry for cleaning and I could use a towel and soap. What is going on with Richard? I send him special greetings and am closing for today. Be so kind and write to me from time to time.

Sincerely, Your Mietek

While the Jewish community of Zbaracz was forced to accept increasingly harsh directives, its burial ground had been overlooked. This situation required immediate attention. Besides living Jews, the already deceased ones had to be dealt with. So as to accomplish this vital task, students from the local Ukrainian gymnasium were called upon to form a special group. Armed with shovels and axes, they marched while singing gay tunes to the Jewish cemetery. Their assigned task was to destroy the gravestones. This work appeared to be a most refreshing form of physical exercise. Several days later, inmates from a punishment camp came here to reduce the toppled headstones into smaller fragments. These were then utilized as paving materials for streets. Most of them had been neatly arranged so that many of the Hebrew inscriptions remained quite visible.

A frightening event took place on September 9, 1942, when the local SS brigade demanded a delivery of 250 Jews. This heinous order caused us to feel like cattle on its way to a slaughterhouse. Our chief representative, Mr. Gruenfeld, started to fulfill his duty by compiling a new roster of death candidates. As expected, the name of every poor devil who was considered to be a liability appeared on the list. Those who could not find good hiding places had no alternative but to accept his or her ultimate destiny. These wretched pariahs had absolutely no chance of escape. The selected victims were herded into the public bathhouse which served as a way station for the death candidates. Whenever certain individuals failed to report as ordered, the tally remained deficient. In such cases Jewish and Ukrainian militiamen were called upon to apply harsh methods in arresting people. While engaging in searches they usually encountered empty streets. This time, no more than one man and his wife were ensnared by the dragnet. The man carried a small child in his arms while the woman shed tears of bitter despair. Witnessing this tragic scene disturbed me greatly but stark events such as this now occurred frequently.

A motor vehicle, which drove up unexpectedly, halted in front of a nearby house. I looked on in astonishment as the notorious SS leader Mueller, accompanied by Mr. Gruenfeld, jumped out and embarked upon a search for the missing old

Mr. Shapu. It seemed as though they were determined to find him, but this astute man discovered an excellent hideaway and could not be found. So as to gather the number of souls called for, other people who were not listed had to be seized.

Unprecedented events took place quite often in Zbaracz. An assortment of communal workshops, known as *Artils,* included various trades. Shoemakers, tailors, hairdressers, and several others were included among these artisans. The shoemakers, who received many orders, nurtured great hopes of being kept busy indefinitely. They produced and delivered good quality shoes and boots to many different clients including SS officials. These privileged individuals ordered the creation of fashionable boots for themselves and their female companions. Judenrat members opened a store where they sold basic foodstuff. Bread, flour, salt, beets, ersatz coffee, shoepolish, as well as other needed items were available. Their prices, however, were considerably higher than in Aryan stores. Early on a loaf of bread weighing 80 grams was sold only to customers with ration cards. Later, the same item was limited to 50 grams and finally to a mere 30 grams. Ultimately, all Jewish-owned ration cards were declared to be invalid.

The German farm supervisor Pfeiffer had a need to impress everyone by strutting about with a riding crop in his hand, apparently in imitation of Julius Streicher the well-known Jew hater from Nuremberg. The land commissar Von Brauschweig and the postmaster Wihan also derived satisfaction by intimidating the local population. Whenever Von Brauschweig, after having consumed large quantities of alcohol, fired his pistol into the night sky people cowered in fear. This obnoxious reveler with his lethal instrument had already terminated the lives of several human beings and all victims were Jews. Among them was Mr. Schurek, the barber, and several of his kinsmen. The Judenrat leadership deemed it expedient to entertain certain officials of the German *Ortskommando* (Local Command) even though they issued orders for the killing of Jews in this area. Whenever such gatherings took place the revelers consumed good food and large quantities of beer. Events such as these happened to be costly affairs, but they held out a promise of prolonging one's earthly existence.

Now there remained a mere twenty-three people in my building. In expectation of an early eviction, it was most difficult for us to decide how we could save our lives. After lengthy deliberations we opted to construct a secret bunker within the confines of this house. To realize such a task we selected a windowless chamber, located at the side of our hallway. We closed up its door and stacked several pieces of furniture in front. We assumed that strangers would be unable to notice anything unusual. We fashioned a small opening near the bottom of this wall which permitted us to crawl from my flat into the chamber. Then, we carefully concealed the entrance so that intruders would encounter difficulties in finding it.

After having survived the initial Aktion we were determined to remain extra alert during the nocturnal hours. Two of us always stayed awake, but this effort proved to be most tiresome. Whenever we detected indications of an imminent police raid, a retreat into our secret bunker was called for. Within the confines of the dark and cold space we endured great discomforts. Especially the children presented major problems. Their coughing, crying, and loud breathing threatened to bring about a sudden demise for everyone. The question of ameliorating the distress of our youngsters produced an excessive mood of anxiety.

In the meantime young Mr. Oehl was inducted into the Jewish militia. Having been assigned to night duties he usually learned about planned events ahead of time. Since his wife and daughter, Noemi, together with his parents-in-law stayed inside our shelter, he tried hard to alert us in time. Every so often one of us felt unwell or fell asleep in the hideaway. Such people had to be roused to keep them from snoring. A pail, utilized as a chamberpot, was an indispensable implement in the bunker. Some of us needed to use it often since the stressful circumstances affected our physical functions. We sat within this narrow space and endured the sheer endless nights with difficulty until the great test came for our hideout.

The dreadful event occurred on October 20, 1942, while young Mr. Oehl was on duty at the Judenrat office. It happened to be my turn to observe the street when a motor vehicle halted near the Ukrainian militia headquarters. I heard someone shouting in German: "Where can we find the Judenrat building?" I noticed the presence of several SS officers who wore white overcoats as they alighted from their machine. The sight of these Nazi fanatics caused me instinctively to become alert. I said to myself: "Now things will become serious." I quickly roused old Mr. Oehl and the other tenants so that they could retreat into the bunker. Young Mr. Oehl then camouflaged its entrance with broken pieces of furniture and walked over to the Judenrat office. Before retreating into the hideout we opened every door in our house to give the impression that this place had already been scrutinized. Mr. Oehl returned shortly and informed us about the presence of a large contingent of well-armed German SS soldiers. They ordered Jewish militiamen to participate in the impending raid.

Previously, able-bodied Jewish men joined the militia so as to gain a measure of useful employment. They did not anticipate the evolving situation which would oblige them to obey all orders issued by the German despots. These men tended to experience severe emotional conflicts, but now they could no longer distance themselves from distasteful activities. There were those Jewish militia members who conducted themselves in a disgraceful manner. I cannot find suitable words of contempt for Mr. Gruenfeld and several of his close associates. These men tried to save their own skins at the expense of others. Even so, destiny now presented us with an entirely new set of circumstances.

Faithless conduct evolved infrequently. At some locations, Judenrat and militia members who refused to indulge in brutal behavior opted to terminate their own lives. I received information about an unusual event that took place in Tarnopol. There, an elderly man approached the execution site while standing erect and composed. He wore a tallit draped over his head and shoulders and conveyed a simple message: "From dust you came and to dust you shall return!"

It is no simple matter to describe how we felt while hiding in this dim enclosure. We sat there for many hours while gasping for air with lumps in our throats. We heard a sudden commotion that soon increased in volume until it reached our opened housedoor. The agitation began to reverberate through our room, but we remained absolutely still. Fearing that the slightest noise would reveal our presence, we felt as if having descended into a trance. While trying to subdue our breathing the weaker ones among us nearly fainted.

The search for victims seemed to go on forever but eventually the commotion died down. Even so, we exercised caution while awaiting young Mr. Oehl's return. He came at six o'clock in the morning and, according to a pre-arranged signal, he knocked three times on the wall. He advised us to stay in place since the current quota of victims had not yet been filled. Later in the morning we noticed that the ongoing manhunt increased in ferocity. The determined SS soldiers formed a dragnet, designed to snare victims that included children and senile people. The few Jews who had remained in their places of lodging were now forced to join those who preceeded them. The ones who remained within secure places of concealment succeeded in evading the dragnet. The SS men also recruited members of the Judenrat to aid them in pursuing their depraved activities and they wore blue armbands inscribed with the word *JUDENRAT.*

Due to a constant lack of fresh air in our retreat, we struggled against the threat of fainting. With the passage of time breathing became ever more difficult in this narrow space. I assumed that the elderly professor, who was nearly deaf, could not comprehend the transpiring events. He appeared to be nearing the end of his life while lying on the stone flooring. Another man appeared to be overpowered by the prevailing turmoil since he fell asleep and snored incessantly. We needed to rouse him but he soon fell asleep again. While staying close to each other we felt extremely uncomfortable. During this prolonged time of tension I began to worry about my deteriorating physical condition. Intermittent spasms of pain in my bladder caused me to feel debilitated.

Mr. Oehl returned to us at noon and said that the danger had passed and we could now leave this narrow space. I then visited Dr. Landau to obtain medical treatment. Upon verifying my severe weakness he was eventually able to help me. Having been forced to wear soiled clothes for a long time, I felt extremely uncomfortable. Some other people with whom I shared the hiding place also found it difficult to walk in a normal manner. When this Aktion ended, the Zbaracz ghetto presented a dreadful appearance. Even though the quota of victims had been filled, the surviving residents still remained out of sight whenever this was possible.

Some one thousand Jews were forced to leave Zbaracz. Later on I learned about their destiny from a statement presented by Mrs. Weinsaft, the local dentist. This woman had succeeded in saving herself in a most daring manner. This is what she said:

SS soldiers came to arrest me at six o'clock in the morning while I still wore house slippers. They demanded to know what I was doing in front of the house at such an early hour. While being led away one of the soldiers remarked: "This one does not even wear her shoes!" One of his comrades added: "For the Rollkommando she surely will not need them!"

Upon arrival at the assembly area we were ordered to sit on the bare ground. The soldiers then herded us into the public bathhouse which was too small to accommodate so many people. The SS troopers then resorted to brutal methods in an effort to squeeze all of us in. Many people screamed loudly. Many children were crushed to death, so that some ended up standing on their corpses. We remained inside that place for an hour until they released us. Then we walked two kilometers towards a waiting train consisting of closed freight cars. We reached the area at nine o'clock in the morning, and then the Germans ordered us to sit on the bare ground next to a railroad track. The soldiers watched us continually as we sat there with lowered heads. Anyone who dared to look up received a swift blow on the head and shoulders. Near midday we were given a ration consisting of bread and water. Initially the guards permitted us to relieve ourselves in a nearby hut until the dreaded SS *Sturmführer* Mueller arrived at the scene. He appeared to be angry and began to shout: "Where do you people think you are? A use of the toilet is forbidden; do it in your pants like at home!"

We were forced to endure unrelenting physical and verbal abuse until the late afternoon when the officer in charge announced that we were about to embark upon a journey. All men between the ages of sixteen and forty were sent with a different transport to a labor camp located in the vicinity of Lvov. All others were consigned to a so-called *Vernichtungsanstalt* (extermination establishment). The guards shoved these luckless selectees into the freight cars, each of which contained a bucket filled with water and three loaves of bread. A battery of bull's eye lanterns illuminated the entire loading area and this provided the stark scene with an almost festive appearance.

I entered one of these cars and nearly fainted. This cage on wheels had no windows with the exception of an opening near the ceiling. This air vent, as we soon realized, was closed up from the outside. While a full moon illuminated the landscape a worrisome mood overpowered me. My father stood nearby as the train started to move at a very late hour. We shared our strong feelings of anxiety concerning the welfare of my mother. If only she were with us we would have been prepared to give up our lives more easily. The prevailing mood of sheer desperation motivated us to attempt an escape. Since we already knew what was in store we were prepared to risk such a venture. One fellow passenger told us that he owned a pocketknife and would gladly give it to us. This handy tool enabled my father to pry open a closed air vent until it was wide enough for one person to squeeze through.

My father and I were determined to vanish at the first opportunity. As soon as the train slowed down I pulled myself up, squeezed my lean body through the aperture, and landed in the grass. My father lost no time in following my example. Barbed wire remnants injured us slightly, but we tried to ignore the stinging pain. While struggling to return to Zbaracz under these dire circumstances, we disregarded our injuries. Since I wore only houseshoes at that time, I staggered along at a slow pace. Other captives who succeeded in breaking out died after having sustained more serious injuries.

A young man from Zbaracz in the Lvov camp was tortured to such a degree that he begged to be shot. Bonnse, his wife, and his daughter were also captured. Bonnse was put on the train to the camp and jumped off again. From the other train his daughter jumped also and then the mother. But she could not find her child. She paid a farmer a large amount of money in order to be taken back to Zbaracz. The farmer took her immediately to the Ukrainian militia. There Mrs. Bonnse was shot right away. In the meantime the twelve-year-old child arrived back in Zbaracz where she met her father.

Mietek sent an urgent message to inform us about his having been infected with typhoid fever. He begged us to supply him with a vial of poison. We thought that, under the circumstances, Mietek's request was justified. We heard that SS soldiers often killed bedridden patients while Aktions were in progress. Janina begged our Judenrat chairman to give her a permit to visit her son in Tarnopol and he agreed to do so. There she soon realized that vital aid was unattainable, and after spending a few days with Mietek she returned to Zbaracz with a broken heart.

[4]

The German authority in Zbaracz decided to create a regular ghetto on October 25, 1942. So as to realize this plan it evicted all Jews from the town and relocated them to a very unpleasant nearby location in the vicinity of the old horse-trading market. The townspeople habitually carted their refuse to this vermin-infested site. Soon after arriving there we needed to build latrines. Our completed facility included no more than a few wooden planks placed over a shallow ditch and a worn-out bucket. Due to the prevailing heat of summer, swarms of aggressive flies and gnats infested this new place of confinement. Every Jew had to vacate his habitation in Zbaracz within twenty-four hours and the Jews who lived in Podvoloczyska also came to join us. There hardly existed enough huts in this place to accommodate all the arrivals. Sometimes twenty people had to find spaces in one room. Since we had a very limited supply of food, it became most imperative to trade our furnishings for something to eat. The local peasantry took advantage of our plight when they descended upon us in large numbers, similar to carrion-seeking vultures, and carted away our last possessions. Recognizing our helpless position they offered us little in return. Initially, this open ghetto was in a desolate state, and we needed many days to cope with our new situation. Broken pieces of furniture remained standing near the shacks while scattered piles of straw and horse dung abounded throughout the area. I continued to make an effort to pursue my usual task of cleaning streets while vainly trying to cope with the present great accummulation of refuse. Peasants from the surrounding area came to seek out useable items and took away whatever they found. Some of these unfriendly people told us: "You should be glad that we give you something for this collection of rubbish. Soon you will be dead anyway!" Many helpless Jews had to endure excessive mistreatments and this caused them to shed bitter tears of despair.

Mietek, who showed up unexpectedly in this newly established site, added additional worries to the already existing ones. Since he was not fully recovered from his typhoid fever, we were allowed to occupy a single hut. The new abode, which served as a shelter for four people, was in a deplorable shape. A corner section of the ceiling hung dangerously low while the dilapidated entrance door might as well not have been there. It was no more than a decrepit barrier that permitted rain and wind to enter freely while an oversized nail served as a doorknob. Even so, we felt content since there was a roof over our heads. So as to dispel moods of despondency we embarked upon the task of cleaning our hut. My good friend Mr. Guensburg gave us several basic pieces of furniture. We also added a cooking pot to our meager inventory of implements.

We knew exactly what awaited us during the next inevitable Aktion. The intentional concentration of such a large number of people left no doubt that the resolve to liquidate us would finally prevail. Our hopes for survival under such dire circumstances dwindled rapidly, and an oppressive mood of impotence hovered continually over us. Certain more vigorous detainees devised strategies for avoiding an early encounter with the Nazi executioners. Even stronger willed people who maintained a resolve to survive lived in constant fright and moved about cautiously.

The better nourished Jewish militia members suddenly acquired a maximum of 130 new recruits. This event reenforced our fear that mass executions would soon be implemented. Mr. Gruenfeld, the despicable collaborator, knew precisely what his Nazi masters expected him to achieve. The local Jews feared his presence as much as that of the SS overlords. The Judenrat nurtured hopes of survival by fully cooperating with the merciless Nazi leaders. Some able-bodied men offered to pay as much as 10,000 zlotys to attain a membership position in the Jewish militia. While being confined within this open ghetto, our day-to-day existence was a frightening one since German SS soldiers, Ukrainian militiamen, and the Jewish auxiliary police made sure that we, poor devils, would not succeed in escaping our predetermined destiny.

The supply of food, put aside for our consumption, was strictly controlled. If alert policemen happened to seize a peasant woman who supplied us with milk, they poured the precious liquid into the gutter. Every so often German and Ukrainian soldiers inspected our dwellings and punished those who had an excessive accumulation of food. These vexations caused us to feel miserable, but soon the Nazis demanded a surrender of watches and money. Tension arose quickly whenever these brutal men entered our district.

Shocking reports of wretched circumstances caused by malnutrition emanated from nearby labor camps. In response to this information, kinsmen of slave laborers set up a workshop for bakers in order to supply the undernourished inmates with bread. The Judenrat insisted that we contribute money to finance this undertaking. We had to line up at tables, and they advised residents about financial contributions. Some of us, due to our condition of indigence, were exempted while others made reduced payments. Since I had nothing to contribute the Jewish militiamen detained me. They vainly tried to squeeze something, no matter how little, out of me. The ghetto police carried out frequent search forays which resulted in several arrests.

Unprecedented events took place in Zbaracz. When Mr. Gruenfeld's daughter married a Mr. Reiss, who headed the local Jewish militia unit, an elaborate wedding feast was staged inside the Judenrat building.

It was strictly forbidden to leave the ghetto perimeter without presenting a *Passierschein* (certificate of passage) for the purpose of obtaining medical aid, made out by the Judenrat. Members of this privileged clique, that included ghetto police-men, were allowed to pass free of charge. Later on, these Passierscheine were doled out under strict supervision. People caught without such a document were consid-ered to be lawbreakers and these were dealt with in a harsh manner. Once the Security Service (SD) office in Tarnopol demanded an immediate withdrawal of all identity cards. After that only cards that were rubber-stamped by that august body were considered to be valid. Any person who was unable to present such a document on demand was designated as an outlaw. Female ghetto inmates also had to obtain identity cards at the German SD office, but many of them were afraid to enter that place. A certain transfer to a punishment camp awaited those who failed to respond as ordered.

When Mr. Gruenfeld took our cards to Tarnopol to obtain a needed SS stamp of approval, he hoped to gain certain privileges. Several days, clouded by moods of doubt, elapsed, since our existence depended upon these absurd ratifications. We speculated about who from among us would actually derive gains from Mr. Gruenfeld's exertions. The long hours of waiting felt like an eternity. This prolonged duration of anxiety tormented our souls since the prospect of an agonizing death inside a punishment camp was in the offing. When Mr. Gruenfeld finally returned, he told us that some cards were not stamped, but still a considerable sum of money was demanded. My own card was priced at 1,000 zlotys. This payment was merely a ran-som for a postponement of one's demise, but no one knew when that would actually occur.

Some men who worked in brickyards, at road repairs, or alongside the railroad tracks soon lapsed into a mood of despair since their identity cards lacked official

stamps. Rapidly increasing amounts of money were offered for the privilege of own-
ing these confirmations. Mr. Gruenfeld, our hard-pressed deputy, embarked upon
another journey to the SD office in Tarnopol, and soon he returned with a fresh
batch of stamped cards. He distributed these valued documents among the lucky
ones who now felt reassured about an indefinite postponement of liquidation. This
nefarious process turned out to be a profitable venture for the eastern railroad
as well. Our exertion shortly degenerated into a repulsive trade in human lives.
Workers struggled desperately to obtain this little stamp which guaranteed a temporary
continuation of life.

While trying to cope with these sadistic torments, there appeared a new regulation. This one demanded that all employed workers needed to acquire an armband,
adorned with the letter *A* (*Arbeiter,* worker), from the Tarnopol labor bureau. This
emblem was obtainable for 500 zlotys.

The Jews of Wiesniovitz, consisting of some 5,000 souls, were all killed in one
Aktion. A local physician together with his wife and child succeeded in saving
themselves by absconding to Zbaracz. While a baptized Jew named Breninger offered
them temporary shelter in his house, he was denounced to the police by an unfriendly neighbor. All of them were then sent to Tarnopol for detention and ultimate
liquidation.

The German SD bureau decided to arrest all Jewish veterinarians who lived in this
area. Initially we assumed that the militia needed their services, but they still ended
up inside a punishment camp. One of these practitioners told me about a meeting of
Polish veterinarians who agreed that there were still too many Jews engaged in this
occupation. Our local animal doctor, Mr. Speiser, swallowed a vial of poison and died
quickly.

Soon additional arrests threatened to crush our remaining emotional equilibrium.
In expectation of harsh treatment we remained vigilant and slept in our street
clothes. Some Jews burrowed cautiously into the soil in an effort to create bunkers.
They even stopped pleading for mercy while hoping to find a measure of security
inside these rough shelters.

Several encounters with dangerous events remain fresh in my mind. One of these
took place during Hitler's day of vengeance on the ninth of November. Every year on
that date we were forced to endure manifestations of great violence. Ever since we
came to occupy this hovel I thought about constructing an underground bunker, but
the realization of such a plan was most difficult. The decrepit hut which served as our
new shelter stood together with several others atop a slightly elevated area. It consisted

of a small room with three obsolete camp beds and a wobbly kitchen table. Several worn-out floorboards supported the length and width of this table. I quickly devised a plan to build a shelter and had a carpenter cut out a section of these planks. The created opening was large enough for one person to squeeze through. When I closed this cover the existence of an aperture remained obscure.

We dug into the soil with an old shovel and removed it in a discarded bucket. Even though we lacked sufficient energy to perform this task, we rested infrequently. Fear of being confronted by our enemies inspired us to make strenuous efforts. We labored in this manner throughout the night even though the disposal of soil-filled buckets presented a serious problem. Fortunately, a heavy snowfall enabled us to cover the removed soil with fresh snow. Militiamen who patrolled the ghetto perimeter shined the beams of their lanterns in all directions, but still we continued to dig with extra caution and gradually progress was made.

The physical condition of Mietek deteriorated steadily, and this caused us to feel alarmed. The helpless youngster, whose legs became swollen, remained in a pitiful state of health. The three of us exerted ourselves in trying to create a large enough space for four people to squeeze in. We also built shelves on either side of this cubbyhole to sit on and placed several wooden boards on top of them. The inventory of our sanctum consisted of a bucket, a candle, and a thermos bottle filled with water.

When the dreaded ninth of November arrived, we expected dire events to occur and remained alert. Mr. Oehl, the Jewish militiaman, came around near midnight and knocked on our window to caution us about an anticipated campaign of terror that was about to start. In response to this timely warning we quickly went underground. Mietek appeared to be extremely distressed and moaned constantly while rising from his bed. We added more bandages onto his swollen legs and then lowered him down into the frigid tomb. When we placed Mietek on a board he must have had a fever of forty degrees Celsius. In the meantime Janina gathered up several vital items consisting mostly of medicines. We created considerable disarray within the hut and left the entrance door open. Finally, Janina and I descended into the dugout and closed the trapdoor above our heads.

The prevailing situation cannot easily be described. While the search for victims proceeded above our heads, we shivered due to overwhelming fright and the chill air. Mietek, who could not find rest, moaned continually while Janina tried to provide comfort by giving him some diluted medicine. During the seemingly endless night I sat in a most uncomfortable position on the remainder of a slab. Late at night we heard the sounds of many voices and the stamping of heavy boots as the Germans entered our hut. We tried to hold our breaths and remained absolutely still. Even Mietek, with his feverish body, recognized the extreme danger. The duration of extreme peril surely determined the course of our immediate future. SS soldiers, who shouted *"Alle Juden raus!"* (all Jews out), now reached our vicinity. Several of them entered the hut and, so as to locate hollow spaces, banged on the wooden floors. Patches of soil rained down upon us as the search continued. The pounding guns were like the knocking of death. Gripped by immense fear of a sudden death we prayed for survival.

When silence returned after the commotion ended, we felt as though we had been granted a new lease on life. As soon as the hunt for human victims diminished in ferocity, an increasing lack of oxygen caused us to feel faint. While struggling to breathe fresh air we slightly raised the cover of our cubicle. This effort brought to our attention the fact that blasts of frigid November air was penetrating the flimsy cabin walls and caused our frail bodies to shiver. We therefore remained hidden inside the bunker until a late morning hour. Upon our final emergence into daylight, we noticed that our shoes and clothes were covered with moist clay. Due to a prolonged exposure to the frigid air, we felt quite numb but we still succeeded in starting a fire. It took us a very long time to dispel the awful chill.

The streets of this ghetto presented a most depressing scene as many distraught people staggered about. There were those who expressed their anguish by emitting shrill sounds while others silently searched for missing relatives. In addition to this great confusion the native rabble arrived for the purpose of carrying out forays of plunder. I watched one young man as he took away a large samovar while a more mature person held onto an assortment of household utensils. Brazen thieves now climbed through opened windows in broad daylight without fear of arrest. Many of the local huts had already been abandoned, and everything was in shambles. Later, a peasant confidentially informed me that some 1,050 people lost their lives.

At the conclusion of this Aktion the occupation authority ordered a closure of all vacated huts. Jewish militiamen carried out this task while gangs of looters still persisted in vile activities. An SD unit led by the notorious SS officer Bischof, who had already earned a bad reputation as a ruthless killer, appeared two days later. He even visited us while enjoying the company of Jadwiga Partyka, his paramour, who happened to be an ethnic German. While members of a rampaging Ukrainian gang carried abandoned objects to the local cooperative storehouse, Bischof, wielding a pistol and horsewhip, embarked upon a private looting foray. Two Jewish militiamen, who served as his assistants, accompanied him. One of them was Gruenberg, the son-in-law of Dr. Halpern, the second Judenrat chairman. The servile Mr. Gruenberg held onto a bottle filled with vodka. Bischof drank from it whenever the need arose to reenforce his sour mood.

We had bad luck when Bischof decided to examine our place of lodging. Before doing so he ordered his entourage to remain outside. This diabolic individual confronted us at once and demanded to know: "Why are you still here? You should have already been resettled with the others!" I knew that the term *Aussiedlung* (resettlement) always referred to eventual physical liquidation. While standing at attention I dutifully replied: "I am still here because of a work assignment!" Bischof then noticed the presence of a bed and saw Mietek who was lying in it. He inquired: "Why is this man lying here?" Janina gathered sufficient courage and spoke out in her son's behalf: "He is one of the workers but now he is ill with a swollen leg!"

We already knew that bedridden captives were often done away with on the spot. Bischof turned to me once again and demanded to see my identity card. He took hold of it and examined it thoroughly. Then he told me to empty my pockets. Every so often the agitated inquisitor brandished his whip close to my face and threatened to use it if I dared to hesitate in complying with his order to place everything I had on the table. The brute relieved me of my wallet, a silver watch, a fountain pen, several postage stamps, and a valueless ring. The loss of this ring caused me to feel special grief since it was a relic of my mother who passed away long ago. As a final gesture of humiliation Bischof cut open the seams of my jacket to make sure that nothing had been sewn into the lining. To conclude this predatory incursion he went out to gather several of his underlings and then instructed them to carry out a thorough search throughout this miserable shack. The subordinates went to work and tossed useable articles of clothing and shoes onto a bedsheet. Several days before Janina had knitted a sweater for a Christian client, but now she was forced to part with her limited supply of wool. Later, Dr. Matinian, the local dentist who had placed the order, implored Bischof to relent in this matter. As expected, the Nazi brute denied his request with the admonition: "It is not proper for a Christian to provide a Jewess with work!"

While Bischof was still in our hut he insisted upon standing on one of our rickety chairs so as to examine the top of a cupboard. While doing so he lost his balance and fell backwards. Fortunately for him I caught his body in my arms. Bischof then glared at me and interjected sarcastically: "I bet you would have been happy to see me croak!" While standing at rigid attention I replied: "Herr Kommandant, we really are not such people as you might think!"

Miss Jadwiga Partyka habitually accompanied Bischof while he participated in anti-Jewish forays. She is reported to have fired shots at Jews.

By chance we survived once again but our joy was severely dampened when we heard about the death of so many of our people who still hoped for a miraculous delivery. My good friend Professor Mueller was among them. In the meantime the weather turned quite cold and frosty. Since I had no opportunity to prepare myself for the cold winter, the assigned duties as a street sweeper could not be carried out. Besides, the ongoing violence prevented me from maintaining proper sanitation. While trying to fulfill my obligations for an entire day, I contracted an inflammation of the lungs. This calamity forced me to remain confined to my bed for nearly three months. Dr. Kamelhaar examined me almost daily. Janina kept me in the dark about the gravity of my illness; she hid from me the fact that I had pneumonia. Due to the enforced inactivity I felt depressed. While lying there I wracked my brain trying to invent a means of escape. I finally concluded that it would be best to disregard this matter and leave it to providence which had aided me until now. A nimble family of mice ran along the rafters above my head. Sometimes one of these tiny creatures jumped down on my bed and then on the floor. In an effort to pass the short daylight hours, I chased them away with a stick but my gloomy thoughts could not be dispelled.

Several noteworthy events occurred in this forlorn area. After our Judenrat chairman, Mr. Gruenfeld, had been sent to Tarnopol, he was replaced by Mr. Shmajuk. Even so, Mr. Gruenfeld returned often in the company of several militiamen. He intended to acquire booty as well as improve his standing with the SD office in Tarnopol. He brazenly demanded a number of items from our Judenrat, and these included a horse, several geese, and an assortment of alcoholic drinks. In return he offered to provide entertainment. In the end he also asked for financial contributions.

Candidates for augmenting the punishment camp population were still available in large numbers. Arrests were carried out any time of the day or night while people slept in their beds or walked in the streets. Jewish militiamen had to watch over these unfortunate ones until the required quota was filled. Mr. Rockita, an official from Tarnopol who had earned a reputation of being a strict camp administrator, visited our town frequently. His escort consisted of a team of Jewish policemen. He impressed me as being a ruthless man who, according to rumor, ordered anyone who could not perform heavy labor to be killed. Their corpses were lying near the Judenrat building. I noticed the body of a woman who had begged for the release of her husband among them. The petty tyrants of our Judenrat devoted considerable time to compiling lists that included many indigent souls selected for physical liquidation. Whenever condemned individuals could not be located, a kinsman was arrested in his stead.

Even though few inmates of punishment camps were able to return, there existed the possibility of gaining a release by paying a large sum of money. Mr. Rockita, as expected, took advantage of the prevailing situation and became engaged in such financial transactions. A practice of dealing with the lives of helpless people soon evolved into remarkably sinister performances by vicious camp leaders, members of Judenräte, and militiamen. The latter often applied a cunning method by appearing at an early hour without wearing armbands. This ruse allowed them to seize large numbers of unsuspecting victims. Ghetto dwellers were also coerced into parting with their clothing, furniture, and provisions. Whenever the ruthless Mr. Rockita appeared together with his mistress, who happened to be a Jewess, a room had to be vacated to accommodate them.

In the meantime my state of health improved somewhat, but I still felt quite weak. My doctor, Mr. Kamelhaar, applied various methods in an effort to restore my health even though he had no access to medicines. Two good friends of mine visited me often. One of them was Munio Schmajuk, a nephew of the current Judenrat chairman. This unfortunate man could no longer laugh since he had been traumatized by the loss of his parents, sister, and wife. The other man was Igo Günsberg, who was released only recently from a punishment camp where he experienced severe hardships. He recently came back to us for a reunion with his wife and Polonia, his four-year-old daughter. His parents, all his brothers, and sisters, and his brother-in-law with their granddaughter had been killed.

Presently, the remaining Jews in Zbaracz anticipated with trepidation various acts of violence. It was most distressing for me to see my compatriots in a mood of despair, and in spite of my own debilitating condition I tried to console them. Once Munio came to visit me and spoke about impending dire events. Mr. Gruenberg, escorted by a squad of militiamen, had returned from Tarnopol. He tried to reenforce sagging spirits by delivering a rousing speech and then distributed ample quantities of alcohol to his policemen. The inhabitants of this ghetto waited impatiently for the expected storm to descend upon them.

In view of visibly increasing tensions I decided to retreat into the secret bunker without delay. Due to my poor state of health it was difficult to accomplish this task. Feeling worn-out, I reclined on top of my wooden board and stayed there. Two young persons, a man and a woman, who had been visiting, followed me into the hidden shelter. Since the small space could not hold more than four people, Richard decided to go back to his workshop at the brick factory. There, so as to avoid being arrested, he hid himself inside a chimney. Now there was one person too many in our bunker, and when I pointed this out to the newcomers they withdrew at once. Due to their presence our place of refuge had now been deprived of its value. The sudden flight of these intruders enabled Janina and Mietek to join me, but before doing so they created a semblance of disorder inside the hut. Finally, they opened the front door and deposited a pile of rubbish next to the the bunker entrance.

Soon after we settled down some strangers who spoke loudly entered our hut. I instantly recognized the voice of Mr. Balin, a militiaman. The despoilers remained inside the room for an uncomfortably long time. We really deceived ourselves by supposing that the worst was over. It happened that several additional militiamen came at five o'clock in the morning. They approached the entrance to our hideaway and quickly tossed the broken table aside. While they banged their clubs on the floorboards we assumed that most likely the previously rejected pair had revealed the secret of this bunker to the militia. This disclosure now posed a threat to our very lives. Finally, these militiamen opened the lid and told us to come out. Janina climbed up first and Mietek followed her.

Overcome by weariness and having lost the will to live, I remained stretched out on my pallet. Due to the unavoidable arrest of Mietek, Janina shivered with fright. Driven by a mood of desperation, she fled directly to the Judenrat office and tearfully begged for the release of her son. While having been left behind in this frigid pit, I lapsed into a despairing mood. It was impossible for me to dispel depressing thoughts concerning my survival while a sudden chill, caused by a fever attack, wracked my body. There existed a dim hope of evading my ultimate destiny but the expectation of being wiped out instantly by a well-aimed bullet was more in accord with the present situation. On the other hand I now faced the possibility of gradually lapsing into a state of unconsciousness and eventual death. I also nurtured an increasing fear of being buried alive in this pit. The narrow entry shaft resembled the neck of a bottle, and I represented the cork that had been pushed through it.

While feeling fatigued after having been ravaged by attacks of nausea and fever, I now assumed that it was no longer possible for me to escape from this ready-made grave. Suddenly, contrary to expectations, five militiamen arrived and they descended into the pit. They took hold of my large frame and tried to maneuver it through the shaft. A most resolute effort, made by these healthier men, seemed to be fruitless. Eventually, they succeeded in placing my body on the bare wooden floor. After being hoisted up once again I found myself lying on the bed that had been left standing in our shanty. Since no SS soldiers appeared in this vicinity, the people who wished to save my life sent for a physician.

Whatever remained in this room had been ransacked, and even Mietek's wristwatch was gone. Besides, our entire food supply as well as 300 zlotys kept for an emergency had disappeared.

One of our physicians volunteered to examine Mietek at the Judenrat headquarters, and it was determined that he still had not recovered from his typhus infection. Being incapacitated by fever he was unable to carry out his duties. Since the militiamen in Tarnopol stole Mietek's meager possessions, we lodged a complaint with Mr. Gruenfeld. He assured us that all pilfered items would eventually be found and returned to the rightful owner, but this promise remained unfulfilled. At the conclusion of this raid we praised God for permitting us to live on. With the severe traumatic experience behind us, we rested inside our hut while contemplating our nebulous future.

While this grave matter dominated our thoughts, the entrance door was pushed open and an absolutely strange-looking man came in. We cowered in fear while this phantom stood in the twilight until it began to speak. Janina quickly realized that the specter was merely Richard, her own son. She did not dare to embrace him since the boy was entirely covered with soot.

This is how it happened. The director of the brick factory had put him in the chimney when the action started in order not to be drawn into this matter himself. Therefore Richard became acquainted with the tasteful wallpaper of the chimney. He looked terrible and funny at the same time. His white wool jacket had become pitch black. We could not get it clean again and it had to be dyed later. Richard himself could be cleaned only with a lot of effort, soap, and use of brush.

I prayed that Christine, who still lived in Munich, would somehow find a way to rescue us before it was too late. I shortly dismissed the idea of her coming to visit us in this forsaken place as absurd and tried to consider some other means. Being an infirm and weak human being, I could not possibly visualize the course of my immediate future. So as to put things in order, while lying on this worn-out mattress, I decided to place my ultimate destiny into the hands of Providence. Having told Janina that my present situation offered no hope of survival, she agreed with this conclusion. It became obvious that the strategy of our captors was to continually diminish the number of ghetto residents until none but the hardiest were left. Even Mr. Schapu, the cunning old fox who managed to save himself until now, was counted among the latest victims. His time had run out. If God has determined your end, you can do what you want but you do not escape your destiny. The case of Schapu made that very clear.

While suffering from energy deficiency I remained stretched out on my bed. The precise date was January 8, 1943. Suddenly, someone wearing a fur coat opened the flimsy cabin door and stepped in. I thought I was hallucinating when I beheld Christine's face. In order to be sure I was wide awake, I slapped my face; however, my eyes did not deceive me. The person who now approached my sickbed was truly Christine and not an apparition. We looked at each other without saying anything. There evolved an interval of silence and then Christine, the loyal soul, spoke words of comfort. She had intended to aid me while disregarding predictably severe hardships. Mr. Matinian, the local engineer, had escorted her to this awful place of lodging. Not wishing to arrive empty-handed Christine brought along provisions and vital articles of clothing.

I could hardly imagine how Christine succeeded in overcoming the many obstacles in reaching this location. She spoke of having devised a plan to visit me some time ago and was determined to carry it out. One of her acquaintances, a Mr. Wand, was an influential official who happened to be in Radom, Poland. She sent him a confidential letter in which she explained my predicament and then posed the question: "What would you do in a case where human lives were at stake?" He replied: "I would surely try to help!"

This favorable response motivated Christine to transform her plan of action into reality. Mr. Wand expedited affairs so that she received permission to proceed as far as Warsaw. German civilians in Poland had restricted access to travel permits, and her chance of going further appeared to be slim. Since Christine was determined to reach me she applied strenuous efforts to overcome hindrances. She encountered exceptional difficulties in Lvov before traversing an additional distance of 170 kilometers to Tarnopol. She continued her journey by boarding a crowded train, but due to the bitter cold weather it arrived there at a very late hour. At that station Christa learned that snowdrifts blocked the single track that led to Zbaracz. In Tarnopol it was difficult for her to find a decent place of lodging near this station, but for her a retreat from this mission was out of the question.

Christine, being unswerving in her determination to cover the remaining 29 kilometers, returned to the station at an early hour. There she encountered two German soldiers who needed to be in Zbaracz. These capable men obtained permission to requisition a locomotive. They shortly set out, together with Christine, upon a hazardous journey into a snow-covered landscape. The prevailing low temperature caused Christine to feel chilled, but she arrived at the Zbaracz terminal in relatively good spirits. She said farewell to the soldiers who took her along and then tramped toward the residence of Dr. Matinian. He already expected her arrival but not under these bizarre circumstances. While Christine sought to regain her strength inside a heated room, Dr. Matinian informed her about what was happening in his town. He expressed serious doubts about my ability to survive the ongoing hardships. Dr. Matinian said that he looked into our hut several days ago and found it deserted, but he could hardly imagine that we had gone into hiding.

When Dr. Matinian escorted Christine into our district he was very surprised to find us among the still living souls, but she was dismayed to find me in such an infirm and bedraggled condition. Christine sat near my bed and tried to comfort me. She remained in Zbaracz for three days, and during that time we talked about shared events of the past and current misfortunes. Daily at dusk, Mr. Schmajuk and Dr. Kamelhaar escorted Christine to the home of Dr. Matinian where she spent the nights. Once she wanted to inspect our secret bunker but afterwards she felt dismayed. Mr. Wand, Christine's reliable collaborator, discreetly agreed to function as a relay station for sending me money by way of Dr. Matinian. This remarkable effort helped to secure our immediate survival since we received enough funds to satisfy local demands. The alloted time passed quickly and I sadly anticipated the departure of my noble visitor. A local peasant, hired by Dr. Kamelhaar, conveyed Christine across the frozen countryside back to Tarnopol with his horse and sled.

We felt a great void after she had left us. My thoughts accompanied her on her journey. I prayed that she would return safely and send us good news soon. After Warsaw she would have an easier trip home.

My downcast deliberations during this unexpected visit had a disquieting effect on Christine during her return journey to Munich. The most difficult segment of this venture turned out to be the one from Tarnopol to Warsaw. Weeks later she sent me a report about this unusual event which included an opportunity to witness the harsh treatment of Jews in Warsaw. Upon Christine's arrival in Munich she felt ill and depressed. Her description of what transpired in Warsaw confirmed the reports that emanated from Zoltan. These accounts enabled me to visualize the magnitude of suffering which the entrapped Jews had to endure. Christine beheld the many emaciated people who appeared in the streets. The stronger ones among them persevered for a long period of time.

We soon received several parcels and money from Christine, and her exertions enabled us to regain some measure of energy. The Germans continued to select candidates for mass murder, and lately even cleverly prepared places of refuge offered scant protection. Relatives were often forced to serve as hostages until the sought after individuals presented themselves at the Judenrat office. There ensued a sudden panic when it became known that all men above the age of fifty were scheduled to be shot. Mietek, who suffered from a swollen leg, was in no condition to perform hard labor. In order to avoid the anticipated selection, he decided to join the militia. In an effort to accomplish this he sold his remaining possessions. This expedient affected our emotions, but we realized that Mietek's life would surely be terminated if he failed to do so.

A sizeable force of Ukrainian militiamen, led by a German police unit, showed up to surround the ghetto. Permission to leave the ghetto area was given only to those who could offer proof of having an outside work assignment. This strict enforcement of regulations indicated that a drive to reduce the local Jewish presence was imminent. Some residents tried to evade capture under the cover of darkness, but most others lacked the will to do so. Since our shelter had been deprived of its usefulness, we needed to exercise extreme caution. The SS soldiers did not know the location of my hideaway, but I feared the presence of Jewish militiamen who knew of the bunker. Due to the current destabilizing situation, we stayed fully dressed, but after several days of waiting the discomforting feeling became almost unbearable. Nevertheless, the need to remain continually alert was most important. We froze in fear whenever several dogs began to bark since their presence indicated that an Aktion was about to start. Mietek, who had gained an advantage by joining the militia, remained on a constant lookout for special SS *Einsatzkommando* soldiers.

All postal services for Jews had already been terminated in many places. Nevertheless, our Judenrat office received permission to continue using them so that messages could be sent out and received. For this special service it had to pay at least double the normal fee. Christine kept sending packages and money. While hiding ourselves in the hut we rapidly approached a state of exhaustion, and by April 6, when it was imperative to be fully alert, we slowly lapsed into a stupor. Mietek, who was not on duty at that time, returned at an early hour. The little mice scurried once again throughout the room and kept me from falling asleep. A mysterious silence, broken only by the occasional barking of a dog, reigned on the outside. Since this could have indicated that an Aktion was in the offing, I started to feel nervous.

A sudden fusillade awoke me at approximately five o'clock in the morning. While still half asleep I arose and peeked through a crack in the door which hardly deserved its name. I beheld a frightening scene where panic-striken people sought to evade a squad of armed soldiers. Years before I had the opportunity to participate in a hunt. What happened on this April morning reminded me a lot of that event. I quickly alerted Janina and Richard since due to unfolding events we needed to prepare ourselves instantly for whatever was in store. The ongoing pursuit of quarry advanced toward the vicinity of our shack. Loud screams emanating from various directions convinced us to descend, together with Mietek, into our mean place of sanctuary. Due to the excitement I forgot to wear my shoes and now I stood on the cold earth with bare feet. This stressful condition caused me to suffer from intermittent stomach pains while cowering inside this dark and frigid cavern.

The shooting spree continued for what seemed to be a long time while screams of anguish emanated from adjacent dwellings. My throat felt dry and the rising blood-pressure inside my head produced a throbbing headache. I felt certain that our demise was near. I only wished that a merciful bullet would quickly terminate my unbearable torment, but an event such as this failed to take place. As soon as the shooting diminished in frequency, I felt more relaxed. Then Mietek wished to investigate ongoing events, and he decided to come out from the underground shelter. Later on he explained that he was obliged to show up at the Judenrat office but warned us not to leave our hut. Before departing he presented us with a bottle filled with fresh water and some leftover bread. He also brought me my shoes and concealed the entrance to our shelter with meticulous care.

Mietek returned an hour later and advised us to remain very quiet. He said that militiamen had received orders to increase their efforts in ferreting out hidden Jews. The SS soldiers had already arrested some 900 fugitives, and Mietek's bride was among them. Even though we felt extremely dismayed it was in our best interest not to show ourselves. Mietek came back to us near mid-day, and he seemed to be in a desperate mood. He tried to gain the release of his bride at a time when shocking events occurred. According to established procedures certain militiamen, upon rendering efficient service, were permitted to request the release of close relatives. They merely had to approach an SS officer and exclaim: "*Ich habe gute Arbeit geleistet!*" (I have performed good work). Thereby Kohanek, the militiaman, one of the more competent subordinates, won the release of his parents, but he had to arrest twenty-four more Jews in return. Kohanek also tried to gain the freedom of his sister, but he could not catch twenty-four more victims.

Previously, while meeting several militia leaders I exhorted them to initiate some means of self-defense, but since they feared massive reprisals nothing came of it. These men, who obeyed Mr. Gruenberg's orders, tried to maintain a semblance of discipline by threatening to confiscate the armbands of newcomers. Sometimes, if they opted to disobey orders, he actually slapped their faces. Mietek returned to us at four o'clock in the afternoon and said that he still waited in expectation of his bride's release. She had already been taken to the train station together with others, and he had to get there quickly in order to save her. Mietek left us alone but the hours of waiting for his return passed slowly. Plagued by evil forebodings, we remained silent but Mietek did not show up. Several hours elapsed before we had to get a breath of fresh air. However, we were afraid to leave our sanctuary. The intermittent sound of machinegun fire was quite audible, and we knew that executions were still taking place. Janina worried herself sick about her son's fate. While attempting to calm her frazzled nerves I reasoned: "Most likely he is now at the Judenrat office," but the unfortunate woman could not be convinced.

We remained hidden for a long period of time until emerging some twenty-four hours later. Richard, acting as a scout, emerged first while Janina and I followed. Apparently, we had survived this roundup, but feelings of anxiety still held us in suspense. We scrutinized the surrounding landscape and noticed the presence of many corpses on top of the fresh snow. A group of local peasants on their way to a market stopped briefly to observe the murder victims. Jewish survivors who expected arbitrary arrests emerged from various places of hiding. Later on we learned that Mr. Sternberg, the commander of the Jewish militia, had also been executed together with forty-eight of his men. Prior to the occurence of this dire event they participated in a gathering of one thousand Jews selected for physical liquidation. Our foreboding of tragedy was confirmed upon learning that Mietek happened to be among them.

Whatever remained of the Zbaracz ghetto resembled a habitation for the living dead while the depopulated huts appeared to be spectral. The wide open doors and windows tended to reenforce this impression. Later, an eyewitness told me that SS soldiers detained the arrested death candidates for several hours next to the public bathhouse and forced them to sit on the bare ground. Several detainees who tried to hide objects of value under the frozen soil were afraid of being searched. Unrelenting SS guards forced these persons to disrobe down to their undergarments and then escorted everyone toward an abandoned large fuel-dumping pit. It was located three miles from the railroad station. This excavation had previously been selected as a convenient site for a mass grave. The condemned souls had to discard their clothes nearby before descending in groups of ten into the pit. The victims were then quickly killed with machinegun bullets.

Many documents owned by the victims had been abandoned next to the bath-house and now a group of children came to collect them. Among these they found photos of my good friend Munio Schmajuk.

There now remained some 900 Jews in this fearful district and very few of them still nurtured hopes of survival. A rumor to the effect that all of us would be termi-nated by April 12 started to circulate. Indeed, several localities within this district had already been rendered *Judenfrei*. I learned with sorrow that my close friend Mr. Guensberg, together with his wife and child, had also been slaughtered. The local populace, eager to get their hands on whatever remained inside the abandoned huts, arrived punctually as expected. Smaller children uncovered trinkets that the deceased Jews tried to hide near the public bathhouse. News of this gainful event spread rapidly and eager treasure gatherers converged quickly upon the site. Several scavengers found more valuable objects.

Many of the still-living Jewish militia members now lost their desire to serve the German *Herrenvolk* representatives and discarded their special armbands. These for-merly good positions could now be obtained gratis. A replacement of Judenrat deputies soon instructed us to gather additional sums of cash. The SS also ordered the establishment of a work detail consisting of able-bodied Jews to close up the execu-tion trench. The layer of soil atop the many corpses was too thin and rivulets of blood began to seep up to the surface. An unpleasant odor of decay now permeated the sur-rounding area. This intolerable situation attracted many stray and hungry dogs. Sometimes these animals carried parts of human bodies or simply bones as far as the edge of town. One dog, owned by a nearby family of peasants, even brought a sev-ered hand into their house. The ongoing process of mass murder severely distressed the remaining Jews and deprived them of any hope of survival.

[5]

few Jews still remained in their houses after the carnage of April 7. Several of us explored a sturdy bunker located in the basement of an abandoned apartment house near the edge of town. This convenient hideaway was accessible only by risking one's life since groups of Ukrainian militiamen patrolled the area. The task of entering this building turned out to be a fearful experience. Mrs. Willner, who had been detained inside the public bathhouse on April 7, happened to be with us. She managed to save her life by hiding within a chimney but her daughter was counted among the victims.

Mrs. Willner informed me about the callous behavior of SS soldiers. She described how one of them confronted the 18-year-old Miss H. and told her: "You are very good looking and because of this I will let you have two bullets!" A pistol shot failed to kill the 22-year-old Mrs. F. While still conscious she pleaded: "In the name of God I want to live on!" The unperturbed butcher shouted: "A Jew does not die, he croaks like a dog!" One of the Nazi executioners confronted a scared five-year-old boy. "Come here little one, I have a bullet for you too," exlaimed the callous murderer before shooting the child at close range.

We stayed for a second night inside this elaborate bunker, which, to our surprise, contained a toilet and electric light. Since its capacity was very limited we searched for a more suitable shelter.

We found a Ukrainian peasant who offered to provide us with a safe hiding place for a certain amount of money. This man, who introduced himself as Mr. Studnitzky, then came for us with a horse-drawn farm wagon to remove whatever remained of our possessions. We also gave him 300 zlotys as a partial payment. The most difficult phase of this venture was yet to come since the penalty for leaving the ghetto without a pass was death. Janina, Richard, and I were willing to take the risk, so we simply walked away from the ghetto even though, due to my recent illness, I could not move along normally. Upon the descent of darkness we simply disappeared from that dreadful environment, and after having gained a reasonably safe distance we quickly removed our armbands. We hardly feared the presence of Jewish militiamen since most of them had already fled into the forest to join a partisan group. The Ukrainian militia, on the other hand, posed for us an increasingly serious threat.

Soon I was overwhelmed by a strong feeling of fatigue and could only move along at a snail's pace. When I stumbled several times my companions needed to assist me in walking. It seemed as if the moon wanted to help us by hiding behind thick clouds. Surrounded by darkness we progressed slowly, but our determination to reach this goal remained strong. Several dogs barked persistently in the distance and this frightened us. Even so we continued to move ahead. At last we saw the outline of a farmhouse, and Richard approached the dwelling while Janina and I sat down under a tree. The Polish farmer, escorted by Richard, soon led us to a nearby barn. We quickly entered this new shelter before our benefactor closed the gate from the outside. Having been left alone we found ample quantities of straw in the semidarkness to lie on. Feeling quite exhausted we reclined at once, but due to the prevailing low temperature sleep remained elusive. The mature son of this peasant visited us around four o'clock in the morning to tell us a clearly made-up story about the expected arrival of an investigation council. He explained that due to this unfavorable situation it was impossible for us to remain here. We felt perplexed and did not know what to do. Later on the old peasant came to see us and explained that he became involved in an argument with members of his family concerning our presence in the barn. Nevertheless, he still wanted to shelter us temporarily.

Mr. Studnitzky's unfriendly wife brought us a pot filled with boiled potatoes and another one with warm milk. Since we already suffered from hunger pains, we ate the precious food quickly. The woman observed us with astonishment, and at the end of our meal she told us not to remain here any longer. She explained that the situation in Zbaracz had now improved, and therefore it was safe for us to go there. We hardly believed this assurance and feared to encounter severe punishments. While Richard reconnoitered the ghetto perimeter, we pleaded with the hostile woman to let us stay here until he returned. Some time later a young girl opened the barndoor and looked in. When she saw us still sitting there, she quickly ran away. This alarming event made us realize that an immediate flight was our best option. No one seemed to notice our departure from the barnyard but we were still afraid of being arrested as fugitives from the ghetto.

Surrounded by the marvels of nature, disturbing thoughts concerning our eventual destiny tormented me. We continued at a snail's pace and upon reaching an intersection of paths I began to gasp for air. Still, I managed to inform Janina that I simply had to sit down in order to catch my breath. Even though she begged me to stand up I was unable to do so. I noticed with alarm the approach of a stranger who most likely intended to confront us. Janina instinctively recognized an unfolding of dire events. In expectation of violence she implored me to stand up but I simply could not do so. The man, whom we expected to become abusive, reached us very quickly. Initially, he looked us over with disdain and then inquired gruffly in Ukrainian: "What are you Jews doing here and where are your armbands?"

Janina replied in Polish, but still a nasty encounter with this belligerent stranger seemed unavoidable. The man who apparently wished to harm us had a gaunt appearance. Not wishing to waste time he snarled gruffly: "Come along with me to the Ukrainian militia!"

We suspected that he merely wanted to steal money or collect a reward for turning us in. While attempting to walk normally I succeeded in taking a few steps. Suffering from weakness I begged the brigand to be merciful and offered to give him all we had to be left in peace. He listened intently to my pleas and then led me into a nearby thicket to avoid being seen by any chance passerby. This unscrupulous robber demanded a mere 1,000 zlotys or a gold watch, but I could give him neither. There ensued an outburst of vile curses and then he stated bluntly: "If you have nothing to give me I shall arrest both of you!"

In anticipation of receiving a veritable death sentence, we pleaded for our lives. Striving to relieve the anger of this stranger, I instinctively began to stroke his stubbly face. The odious extortionist then grabbed Janina's handbag and took from it her last 360 zlotys. Finally, he ordered me to disrobe and then examined me closely but found nothing. This disappointment motivated the robber to release us with the warning not to mention anything about this incident to anyone in the district. While expending a final burst of reserve energy, Janina and I succeeded in returning to the ghetto area without arousing attention.

After having entered our blighted district, we passed a shanty from which emanated joyful singing and laughter. This inconceivable sort of behavior caused us to feel perplexed. Later on we learned that a gathering of young people had taken place there. They previously decided to escape from the ghetto along well-hidden routes so as to join an active group of partisans. They now celebrated this occasion before entering the forest.

Inside our shack there remained no more than two broken beds, several cooking pots, a battered hatbox, and a small suitcase. We intended to use this dilapidated structure merely as a temporary shelter. Our neighbor, Mrs. Kristal, who felt devastated by fear, asked us to allow her together with three small children to stay with us. Soon after we gave her our consent to do so the SS deputies at the Judenrat office ordered us to abandon this ram-shackle hut. We had to comply with this command within twenty-four hours since the ghetto area was scheduled to be reduced. Whatever remained in this locality amounted to a tiny enclave consisting of twenty-six dwellings besides the bathhouse. We now realized that there was hardly enough space for Janina and me.

Mr. Lazarewicz, the local postmaster, who was an ardent postage stamp collector, wished to remain on good terms with me. He recently came across a postcard from Hungary. It was mailed by my brother Lajos who sent me birthday greetings. Mr. Lazarewicz allowed me to read the message but refused to let me keep the card. I also received a most welcome parcel from Christine containing ground coffee beans and a cake. Mrs. Kristal, a native resident of Zbaracz who still maintained friendly relations with some of her former neighbors, stayed with us and she received a cooked chicken from them. This unexpected gift stilled our hunger for some time.

We obtained no instructions concerning the selection of new living spaces during the entire day and so lingered on in our old huts. I observed the surrounding area under the cover of darkness and it appeared spectral. Mrs. Kristal's three small children quickly became adjusted to living inside this primitive domicile, and I allowed them to spend the night in our underground place of refuge. Two strange women shaking with fright knocked on the door at a late hour and implored me to let them come in. In consideration of the prevailing harsh circumstances I allowed them to enter. Close to midnight a rabble, wishing to take advantage of gainful opportunities, invaded our ravaged district. Shadow-like forms scurried from one emptied shack to the next in order to remove all remaining useable items. Some scavengers arrived with carts which enabled them to transport heavier loads. Amidst this hectic activity Ukrainian militiamen tried to regulate the flow of traffic. The Jewish militia could no longer be relied upon to render assistance because their services had now been terminated.

Since the prevailing physical and emotional stress caused us to feel thoroughly drained, we should have been in need of sleep, but somehow this feeling remained elusive. The usually nimble mice stayed out of sight and it seemed as if they had abandoned us. Every so often I peeked through the partly opaque window to observe unfolding events. Amidst the darkness of night someone approached our hut and smashed the entrance door open. Instantly there appeared the outline of a robust man who switched on a very bright lantern and directed its strong beam into our haggard faces. This mysterious intruder then entered without waiting for an invitation. He wore a long overcoat and a cap which nearly covered one of his eyes. We could see the gleam of a lit cigarette in his mouth and noticed that he held a pistol in his right hand. This visitor from hell scrutinized us for several minutes and then slammed the door shut behind him. He advanced several steps toward the middle of our room while shouting in his native Ukrainian: "Why are you here?"

I urged Janina, who shook with fear, to inform the intruder about our expectation of being transferred to a different hut. The ruffian confronted me instead and demanded to know my name and if I lived here.

Since I could not understand nor reply in Ukrainian or Polish, I tried to justify my existence in German. The angry man began to shout but whatever he said remained without an explanation. The vile thug soon realized that nothing would be gained here and he left us in peace. While waiting for the arrival of dawn we could hardly sleep during that anxiety-ridden night.

Having survived the night we entertained the feasibility of staying here. I kindled a fire inside our primitive stove while Janina prepared a most frugal meal. Around midday a combined German and Ukrainian patrol appeared, and its leader ordered us to abandon this squalid place by two o'clock in the afternoon. He also instructed us to occupy one of the previously vacated huts. Professor Halpern, who together with his wife and child came to live in a place which consisted of one room, invited us to join them. He and his family members also sheltered a three-year-old girl whose parents lost their lives during the previous Aktion. Even though we occupied no more than a small corner area we thanked God for providing us with a roof over our heads. We sensed that our precarious existence was deteriorating rapidly, and the noose around our throats felt tighter from one day to the next.

Once again we thought about seeking shelter within the large bunker located beyond the ghetto area, but getting there was a very risky venture. Even so, our bare existence depended upon this and chances had to be taken. We noticed upon returning to the old hut that the place had been ransacked and our remaining possessions as well as the bread had been stolen. Even the window, including its frame, was dismantled. The clever mice also fled to a safer place before the pillage took place.

The date of April 19, 1943, remains etched in my memory. During that fateful day we stayed within the allotted space in our living quarter, but there was hardly enough room to stretch our legs. Since only one narrow bed and a bench had been provided for ten people, we slept in a sitting position. Due to the constant instability we did not take off our street clothes during the night. The dispondent mood of those who occupied the twenty-six huts cannot easily be described. While struggling with overwhelming depressions and nervous tensions, the tenants nearly gave up every hope of survival. Several people carried along small bottles filled with cyanide pellets to bring about a quick demise. Other tormented souls even lost interest in greeting each other; instead they silently shook hands. This lack of verbal communication became very noticeable after the conclusion of an Aktion. Even though the captives took it for granted that their lives would soon be terminated, the sudden appearance of SS soldiers unleashed feelings of panic. I would like to compare it to a chicken coop, from which every now and then a few victims are picked. As with the nightly intrusions of a marten, we would scatter like chickens when our captors appeared.

When we finished consuming our noonday meal consisting of potato soup, I wrote a letter to Christine. While Janina washed the dishes, Mrs. Halpern put on another dress and black stockings. Then she sat on the bench and asked me to summon her husband and the young son who had stepped outside. In the meantime she whispered something to Janina, but whatever she said seemed to be most disturbing. When her husband and son reappeared she implored them to accept her decision to escape quickly from this hopeless situation. She held out her hand to me and said: "I am unable to continue living here and so I must say farewell to you!"

I momentarily failed to grasp the seriousness of this situation. Her husband who appeared confused by what transpired could not utter a single word while his young son whimpered in fright. I too became alarmed and shouted: "You should not have done this!" but my feeble rebuke came too late. Her final words were: "At last I now feel very peaceful!"

Mrs. Halpern soon lapsed into a state of unconsciousness. She had indeed swallowed poison, and this was confirmed when we found the emptied container of cyanide. Since we could not summon a physician we called upon Mr. Schorr and Mr. Schachet, two former chemists, who stood nearby to render aid. Both men attempted to save the life of this poor woman by giving her hot milk and then an injection, but these efforts bore no fruit. Later we constructed a crude wooden casket and placed her body in it. No more than five people received permission to carry the remains of this poor woman to the burial ground. The group of mourners included Mr. Halpern and his son. A simple peasant cart conveyed the corpse while we recited silent prayers.

The fresh soil atop the burial site seemed to quiver occasionally as if the despatched people could not rest in peace. Some able-bodied Jewish men went there at times to pile on more soil.

Mr. Gruenfeld obtained militia reenforcements from the Tarnopol ghetto while the anxiety-ridden mood that prevailed in our shrunken location increased markedly. When Rockita, Mr. Gruenfeld's son-in-law, together with a squad of ghetto policemen, came here we thought that the task of physical liquidation was at hand. We also assumed that the Tarnopol labor camp's continued existence was desired, and many of the Jews who still lived here wished to go there. The Judenrat office announced that a move such as this, which included smaller children, could take place in exchange for a financial contribution. Actually, many of these children were by now either dead or remained hidden by local peasant families, or they were killed by their parents. Mr. Schmajuk, our Judenrat chairman, told me that Rockita demanded the exorbitant sum of 25,000 zlotys for the aquisition of a doubtful new lease on life. Since my remaining funds were quite inadequate, all hopes of reaching Tarnopol had to be abandoned.

Two automobiles arrived in our district during the afternoon. Rockita, who stepped out from the first one, ordered everyone to gather and hear his declaration. He now disclosed a new directive: "Every person will shortly be examined to determine if he or she is capable of performing physical labor." This effort, as it turned out, was merely a scheme to tranquilize us. Rockita explained further: "We shall all gather here once again tomorrow at seven o'clock in the morning!" An outspoken woman dared to address Rockita by asking: "May I go to the same camp where my husband is now located?" Rockita replied: "I may even send you to a camp where many good-looking men are held and then you can select one for yourself."

The Jewish detainees could only guess what awaited them when they assembled at the appointed hour. Professor Halpern who was accompanied by his son decided to bring along a small flask that contained cyanide poison. He said that he would gladly drink it so as to avoid additional torments. When Rockita reneged on his promise to show up again, the persevering gathering soon dispersed. Then several young men declared that they were ready to leave the ghetto perimeter without permission. They hoped to reach the province of Volhynia where they could join a group of partisans. They started out during the night but after entering a forest they walked into an ambush. Four of them were killed instantly while the fifth man, who happened to be young Mr. Hindes, was brought back several hours later by local peasants to the Judenrat building. This unfortunate boy, who could not obtain medical attention, died shortly as well. The Jewish militia leader who anticipated trouble soon released the corpse to relatives.

From now on not a single day passed without encountering distressing circumstances. Once a fourteen-year-old boy who called himself Mannheim was found wandering aimlessly together with his younger sister through our neighborhood. He explained that both parents had recently been arrested by SS soldiers. Presently, a local peasant offered to employ the boy alone for carrying out barnyard chores. This man soon changed his mind since he was not inclined to shelter both children. Other orphaned youngsters tried to fend for themselves as well. One woman who also lived in our ghetto looked after her two grandchildren because their mother was no longer alive. Realizing that these unfortunate people were overwhelmed by depression and fatigue, I invited them to stay with us. One of the offspring implored their grandmother to stop crying and then tried to console her by saying: "Look, I am still alive!"

A squad of Jewish militiamen was sent from Tarnopol to keep us from running away, but its members soon made attempts to squeeze money out of us. Richard became alarmed and instinctively retreated into the hideaway, but his presence there was soon uncovered. When Janina heard about this turn of events she became afflicted with uncontrollable trembling, but the callous militiamen remained impassive. They then demanded a ransom payment of 1,000 zlotys in exchange for Richard's release. We managed to borrow 500 zlotys which the militiamen grudgingly accepted.

While we were enjoying the warming sunshine three Ukrainian policemen appeared in our district. Their presence unleashed a recurring panic among the jittery residents who quickly retreated into their existing places of sanctuary, but I remained standing next to my hut. While these strangers drew near their spokesman approached me and inquired: "Could you tell me how the people who live here are getting along?"

I replied: "All of us live in fear of dying shortly."

The mediator of this group assured me that we had nothing to fear. He explained that he once lived in Zbaracz but his comrades derived from other places in the district. I emphasized the fact that we lived here under dire circumstances. The strangers responded by assuring me that they did not come here to harm us. He and his companions merely wished to see how we fared in this place. I told him bluntly: "If we had not been forced to remain here we would certainly have lived in a normal manner."

The curious visitors then requested permission to examine the interior of our doleful shanty. While harboring doubts concerning the existence of common civility in this disorderly region, I imagined that our encounter was only a dream. I then ushered these unusual guests into my humble abode. They immediately noticed the presence of flowers on the table and several slices of bread. One of them remarked in astonishment: "I see that you do have something to eat here!"

I replied: "We are quite satisfied with small rations; we only wish to stay alive."

Janina then showed the strangers a photo of Mietek and lamented his untimely demise. One of the guests commented: "Your son has it good now; he does not have to endure more torments."

The courteous visitors then thanked us for the interview and proceeded to investigate various other sites in this forlorn district. I imagined that these people were interested in viewing the remainders of a human race in danger of becoming extinct. I also assumed that the unusual visitors had information about what was being planned for us in the imminent future.

In our neighborhood there stood a large house with a well-tended garden, and it now served the Judenrat as a new headquarters. German officials and Ukrainian militia leaders came and went there frequently. They stayed inside this building to be entertained by the Judenrat leaders with ample quantities of spirits. From the vantage point of my window I could clearly see the garden with the brightness of its foliage. Children, who used it as a playground, simulated Einsatzkommando activities by fashioning bunkers with discarded pieces of wood. The youngsters also participated in make-belief camp Aktions by impersonating real events in fanciful details.

A troop of SS soldiers showed up here the following week and stormed into the Judenrat headquarters. The fanatic visitors from hell brutally assaulted the director of this office. They then invaded the nearby Jewish militia billet and severely beat anyone who happened to be present. These heartless demons persevered in entering Jewish dwellings and firing lethal weapons during the hours of darkness.

Janina wished to prevent her son from falling into the hands of the ever-present SS executioners, but due to a paralyzing fear she was unable to do so. It would have been most expedient to provide Richard with an Aryan document, but a large sum of money was needed to acquire one. Due to a steep rise in prices, the funds that derived from Christine and whatever we earned were barely enough to survive on. Our financial distress, however, turned into a profitable undertaking for a well-disposed person. In order to sustain Richard we tried to acquire money in a furtive manner. The one who offered to aid us was a Mrs. Kunicki, a non-Jewish woman who lived in Zbaracz. This woman described her intention to visit a sister who resided in Krakow. There she would certainly be able to gather various items from Janina's former apartment in return for a monetary reward. There still remained a good suit of clothes and a valise from her late husband besides several other saleable items.

Upon arrival at the old abode in Krakow, the current occupants informed our helper that the desired articles were now in the hands of Sophie, the former maid who lived not far away. With the patronage of our acquaintance we now earned enough money to procure a forged certificate for Richard. Mrs. Kunicki's sister who maintained contacts with reliable people was instrumental in procuring the needed document. With a confirmation of Aryan ancestry in his possession, Richard embarked upon a risky journey to Krakow. Initially he walked all alone to Tarnopol without encountering any hindrance. There, Mrs. Kunicki's sister offered him temporary shelter. While on his way to this place Richard had the bad luck of being recognized by a man who once lived in Zbaracz. He intended to denounce him to the authorities, but then he thought it over and embarked upon a different plan. Instead he approached Richard and demanded 5,000 zlotys for keeping his mouth shut. Mrs. Kunicki's sister recognized the seriousness of this situation and gave the extortionist some money. He seemed to be satisfied with the amount. In order to avoid more dangerous confrontations, the good woman accompanied Richard to the train depot. Soon thereafter Janina received a telegram from the local postmaster which informed her about Richard's safe arrival in Krakow. Some time later Janina found out that Mrs. Kunicki and her sister gained additional profits by aiding other Jews in a similar manner.

[The bogus Christian birth certificate was made out to a previously deceased man, named Stefan Vlasovski. Richard's light colored hair also gave him the appearance of a genuine Pole. While the Krakow-bound train halted at the Lvov station near midnight he could not help noticing an unusual brightness in the sky. He quickly recognized this occurrence as a spreading conflagration within the Jewish district. One aroused fellow passenger remarked: "I hope that at last they are getting rid of these annoying Jews!"

As soon as the train gained speed a team of SS soldiers started to search for fugitive Jews and other unwanted travelers. It did not take long until they came to confront Richard. His document was found to be in good order; even so they lingered for an uncomfortably long time in his vicinity. Richard began to experience a growing feeling of anxiety, but still he succeeded in hiding this mood until the grim inspectors finally decided to move on. The train reached the Krakow main terminal at an early hour, and soon Richard strode quickly in the direction of Lobzowska Street, located in the Piasek district. Sophie, the loyal maid, appeared surprised when she saw Richard but welcomed him into her place of sanctuary.]

[6]

While our difficulties multiplied rapidly in the Zbaracz ghetto, the Judenrat leadership distributed placards, adorned with a large Star of David. In accordance with an SS directive these had to displayed at the entrance door of our dilapidated huts. Posted bulletins warned the Christian population to desist from sheltering fugitive Jews. Anyone caught breaking this law would be shot. Placards containing similar warnings were posted in the streets of our town as well. This particular type of intimidation revealed that accelerating efforts to bring about our total annihilation would soon be implemented. Since nearly all conceivable hideaways had already been uncovered, many able-bodied Jews fled into nearby forests. Orders arrived at the Ukrainian militia station to pursue and execute these fugitives wherever they could be found. I also devoted much thought to constructing a bunker within the woodland after discarding various other options as useless.

We soon believed that without a doubt our days in Zbaracz were numbered. Even so, some friends and neighbors attempted to seek my counsel. This severe tightening of the noose, so to speak, produced a most oppressive mood among the inhabitants of this ghetto. Mr. Schorr, the chemist, whom I regarded as a decent human being, told me that all members of his family were now dead and his will to live on was gone. Professor Halpern and his son also visited me. They struggled continually to find a means of escape. Others prepared themselves to disappear within the extensive nearby woodlands.

Time seemed to be running out swiftly for me and Janina, but useful advice remained elusive. Like others, I sensed the presence of great danger and wished to leave this vulnerable place. In an effort to encourage poor Mr. Schorr I told him: "Always remember, no matter what happens God will stand by us!" Professor Halpern asked: "How will our just God save us?" I replied: "This is the creator's big secret which we mortals cannot comprehend."

I struggled instinctively to retain my deep-rooted trust in the justness of our creator while suffering from being submerged in degradation and gloom. Having no place to hide we anxiously awaited whatever was in store. My many silent prayers for salvation were miraculously answered at virtually the last moment on June 6, 1943.

A baker, known as Mr. Lachwicki, who worked in this town offered to provide us with bread and flour in exchange for certain items of value. Initially, Janina was afraid to get involved with this stranger, but I felt inclined to deal with him. While Janina went to weigh our purchase in the place of a neighbor, I revealed our serious predicament to the Pole. Taking advantage of a sudden idea I asked him: "Could you possibly help us in surviving here and thereby save our lives? If so I would give you all the money that is sent to me."

Mr. Lachwicki replied without hesitation: "I am only a baker here and so I am not in a position to help you. I have to support seven children and a wife. Even so I will think about your offer." This unfolding drama appeared to be tenuous. The presence of this man who finally agreed to cooperate with me at practically the last moment indicated that the ruler of the universe had not abandoned us. Due to the fact that the prevailing situation seemed to be without a glimmer of hope for a miraculous turn of events, it was beyond my imaginative ability to determine in what manner our lives could be saved.

When our potential benefactor visited us during the afternoon, we agreed to fulfill his demands. While I gathered up whatever appeared to be of some value, the Pole said that he would soon come back. In the meantime I visited the Judenrat office and petitioned the bureaucrats to provide me with a pass for seeking medical aid. While struggling to subdue a rising mood of anxiety, I waited for Mr. Lachwicki's return, and when he finally showed up his report happened to be quite disappointing. He informed me of the fact that his kinsmen were afraid of getting involved in such a dangerous venture. Janina quickly responded to this bad news by plunging into a despondent mood. This caused me to worry about her ability to persevere. The basing of our hopes on vague promises of deliverance seemed to be an exercise in futility and this began to frazzle me as well. Even the strongest mortal was bound to falter while suffering from prolonged torments. It seemed as if Satan tried to dispel my reliance upon a heavenly intercession, but several hours later this gloomy outlook began to dissolve. I still hoped and prayed that the baker might locate someone who was willing to shelter us.

Mr. Lachwicki returned next morning in a benign mood and told us about having found out about another place of refuge. Janina, upon learning this gathered renewed hope and agreed to accompany him to the site of another sanctuary. Since I could not make myself understood in Polish, I opted to lag behind. Janina now distinguished herself as a most skilfull bargainer while dealing with Mr. Bestetzky, our potential benefactor. This lean and tall man was an advocate of fascism. He now lived in an old mansion where he dedicated his remaining days to tending a magnificent rose garden. Most people who lived in this district assumed that the elderly man was broke, and for that reason he could be persuaded to shelter us in exchange for financial support. We accepted his reasonable demands while Janina impressed him with her excellent knowledge of the Polish language.

Since Janina was unable to walk back to Bestetzky's house again, we had to endure another night in the ghetto, a night which almost cost us our lives. The SS arrived at midnight, and we miraculously survived in our underground shelter.

We emerged from our subterranean shelter at an early hour. Since our permits to leave the ghetto had expired, we needed to apply for new ones. We went to the Judenrat office and there saw a note that was pasted on its entrance door. It stated: "Passes for leaving this area are no longer given out!" Since the permit we carried was the very last one, I kept it as a memento.

Parting from our fellow ghetto inmates whom we left behind turned out to be a very emotional experience. I looked into the sad eyes of Professor Halpern and bid him a silent farewell by shaking his hand. Mr. Schorr, the chemist, stayed hidden in a secret location, but Mr. Sonnenschein, the watchmaker, grasped my outstretched hand and tears welled up in his eyes. He had a somber expression on his face while showing me a small bottle filled with cyanide poison. In a trembling voice he said: "This drink will shortly become my eventual salvation!"

In order to avoid being noticed we distanced ourselves separately from this stark area while expecting to meet Mr. Lachwicki at the agreed-upon location. During our walk to Mr. Bestetzky's residence we were afraid of being recognized as fugitives from the ghetto. Even so, the longed-for goal was reached without encountering difficulties. Our guide led us through an unlocked entrance door into a decorously furnished parlor. After having been forced to live in a most depressing environment, it was difficult for me to cope with this display of fading opulence. An overpowering aura of timelessness abounded here. In stark contrast I saw a well-kept rose garden through an opened window. While the sun shone brightly a delightful fragrance streamed into this outmoded room. Being here I hardly recognized the difference between illusion and reality. While struggling to adjust to these confusing emotions Mr. Bestetzky, the mysterious landlord, entered through a small door.

A large portrait of the Mother of God that hung on the wall distracted my attention and this caused me not to notice the entry of our host. Now I had to think of our Munich angel again, of our Christine, who emphasized in her letter her unwavering trust in God. In one of her last letters she wrote to us of her daily prayers for our liberation and that she was on her knees in front of the statue of the Virgin Mary. As the fear of death would often make me tremble, now it was deep gratefulness for our rescue from the greatest torment.

I needed a brief interval to grasp the reality of this situation and then held out my hand in greeting. This tired-looking man who had a military bearing offered me a formal salute before introducing us to our new place of refuge. The congenial baker had provided us with two loaves of bread before our exit from the doomed ghetto. I now gave one loaf to our host together with my last 1,000 zlotys. Then it was Janina's turn to hand over her dead husband's good suit of clothes.

Wishing to introduce us to our hiding place the landlord, who remained silent, now led us by means of an unsteady ladder into a subterranean chamber. Several paces further on he illuminated with a kerosene lamp an opening in the paved flooring close by the end of this chamber. There we encountered a crude flight of stairs that led into a still deeper vault. This continually dark and silent cavity would from now on serve as a secure place of refuge. When on November 9, 1938, the Jewish stores, including mine, were destroyed, I overheard a Bavarian saying: "It will not get any higher than this." I had to think of this phrase after we had arrived in our clay pit which for who knew how long would be our place of residence. It would have been appropriate to say: "It does not get any lower than this."

While descending further into this obscure cavern, I began to feel uncertain in regard to the promised state of security within this place. My previous euphoric mood now faded quickly while thinking about the hideous fate encountered by the doomed ghetto dwellers. A day later, our imperious host came to tell us that a large troop of SS soldiers had suddenly arrived in Zbaracz. These pitiless troopers, together with Ukrainian militia support, now combed through whatever was left of the ghetto and killed everyone they encountered. This frightening report caused us to remain sleepless during most of the night. Early next morning, while bringing us something to eat and drink, the landlord spoke of having heard much shooting. We thereby realized that the final Aktion was still underway.

After the time of liberation I had an opportunity to interview various survivors of this massacre. One of them was Mrs. Zuckermann. She readily described several violent incidents in detail. Mrs. Schmajuk, the Judenrat chairman's wife, was seized together with her two young children near the Ringplatz. Being unable to find a means of escape she and her son swallowed a poisonous substance. They both died quickly but her daughter, who tried to run away, was shot to death by an SS soldier. Mr. Sonnenschein, the watchmaker, who once showed me his vial of poison was found dead, together with several other Jews, near the old cloister rampart. Mrs. Zuckermann, as well as Professor Halpern and his son, Richard, stayed inside the house of Mr. Bilinsky when the Aktion started until the latter urged them to flee. When they got as far as the bee-hives, Professor Halpern told his offspring to swallow the venom. The distressed young-ster pleaded that he should be permitted to stay alive a little longer. He hoped to find an opportunity to persevere but none presented itself. Since it was no longer possible to postpone the end, he and his father ingested the lethal substance. Mr. Oehl Junior, his wife, and little Noemi, together with Dr. Kamelhaar, located a place of refuge inside the home of a local peasant who seemed to nurture remorse but soon betrayed them to the German despots. Soldiers came quickly and removed the ill-fated ones to a site located near the old castle where they had to dig their own graves. Their lives were promptly terminated with bullets at that site.

The carnage that took place within the ghetto perimeter did not end until late at night. The Nazi executioners performed their assigned task of rendering the district Judenrein in a remarkably efficient manner during June 9, 1943.

Due to this final act of inhumanity we were unable to rejoice about our own eleventh-hour delivery. Instead, we tried to acquaint ourselves with this mysterious sanctuary. While doing so we encountered nothing but cold stone walls. Many hours later our benefactor came to provide us with two worn-out chairs. We used one of them as a little table by placing a hatbox on it. Then the man brought an ample quantity of straw, together with a discarded mattress. A large pitcher, filled with fresh water, completed our furniture. This cellar, so to speak, was merely an antechamber that offered space to loiter every so often. Our living quarter, on the other hand, was located some three meters below. The upper basement area measured three square meters and its height was four meters. A rather unsteady ladder permitted us to climb down through a trapdoor from above. Due to a prevailing summertime high humidity the walls showed stains created by dampness even though the air down here remained at a stable cool temperature. Since the floor of this lower cubicle consisted of moist clay, our accumulation of straw tended to absorb the dampness. While Mr. Bestetzky soon honored us with a visit he could hardly use a match to light a cigarette. The only source of daylight consisted of a twenty-centimeter-wide window, located high up on the cellar wall. It alone permitted some brightness to illuminate this antechamber.

Janina and I, finding ourselves in this subterranean cell, still nurtured hopes of survival. The answer to when and in what manner our molelike existence would end remained unknown. No matter, this place of seclusion restored our faith in salvation. I felt exceedingly grateful to Christine for her efforts on our behalf. While rendering financial assistance she seriously endangered her own life. I wished to believe that the Universal Power had sent Janina to me. So as to strenghten my fortitude he imposed afflictions and privations upon my being. At the time God brought me together with Janina, he put us through trials due to our common religion. He let us both experience the greatest deprivations, tortures, and fear of death; he took away from both of us our relatives; and he kept us alive in often miraculous ways. He sent us both into this cave. It became clear to me that God was holding his shield over us. He wanted us to be together. And therefore we became a pair. Our witnesses were the stark walls of clay, which cried as we did. This miserable bed of straw should become our common resting place.

The moist straw on the bare floor of this wretched cellar often caused us to feel forlorn. I now began to worry about my steadily deteriorating health. I could have no access to medical aid and a doctor's visit would most likely have cost me my life. I had no choice but to come to terms with the prospect of dying and being buried forever within this pit. We now had nothing more than the aforementioned hatbox, a small suitcase that contained some clothes, two soup plates, and eating utensils. I gave the 300 zlotys that remained in my pocket to Mr. Lachwicki who then bought vital provisions such as potatoes, turnips, and bread. Each morning at an early hour he supplied us with a pot filled with hot water for washing ourselves and another one with tea. Every so often the host's wife brought boiled potatoes and some watery soup, part of which we saved for an evening meal.

It should not be assumed that Mr. Lachwicki and Mr. Bestetzky looked after our basic needs for altruistic reasons. Their motive for embarking upon these humane efforts was based primarily on monetary gains. In fact the two Polish benefactors cooperated in fleecing us without compunction. For example, they charged 7.50 zlotys per kilo for bread which usually cost .60 zlotys. Even so, we felt content with having been permitted to stay here. It turned out to be impossible to store anything in this shelter. The bread quickly turned moldy and our writing paper became damp. Our shoes and clothes threatened to disintegrate while sitting on piles of straw.

Because of the prevailing gloom we could hardly familiarize ourselves with these new surroundings but like people afflicted by blindness, we quickly learned to accept our plight. Since the unending monotony and inertia was hard to bear we welcomed the sounds of constantly gnawing rodents. Our whispered conversations soon diminished in frequency and stayed muffled in this austere chamber.

The prevailing silence inside our enclosure caused me to descend ever deeper into an abyss of inertia. This enforced banishment under the earth's surface provided an opportunity to become engrossed in somber reflections.

The night, the best friend, which I have met,
To which I take all my worries and longing,
Is always fresh, as often I embrace it.
And the companion of her dreams, sleep,
Gives me pleasant things, without envy and discreetly.
I am a beggar at the day, a count at night.

The starkness of the day is too petty
And envious of the realm of thought
Knowledge wants to grow upwards;
When Pan blows his flute, then knowledge is mine.
I want to thank you for each hour, night,
Because afterward—I will have to be a beggar again!

With the first day we worried how to satisfy our avaricious host.We could not possibly leave this cellar in order to breathe fresh air. We knew that rewards had been posted for information regarding the locations of hidden Jews. We therefore stayed within the walls of this cellar, even during the night. While the ghetto still existed, venturesome detainees established hiding places within forests, abandoned farm buildings, and inside cemetery crypts. Many such fugitives were discovered and, since no solitary member of the so-designated Jewish race was permitted to survive, they were liquidated on the spot. Once, Mr. Bestetzky told us that due to this situation we had to appreciate his desire to shelter us. This state of affairs motivated him to add several additional wishes. He sat down to compile a new list of demands which Christine was expected to fulfill. This time he even insisted on getting a wristwatch. Whenever money arrived at the Zbaracz post office, he appeared to be momentarily content, but prior to certain holidays he expressed a greater urgency. Since the length of our strict confinement remained unknown, we coped with continual worries.

I fervently hoped that Christine's money transfers would continue to arrive and that Dr. Matinian would retain his interest in playing the role of intermediary. Indeed, when he received 1,000 zlotys, the money went directly into the pocket of Mr. Lachwicki. Needless to say, Mr. Bestetzky did not hesitate to pocket his share of the booty. Once the former benefactor tried to deceive us by announcing that a vital money transfer failed to arrive. Since I then had nothing to give him, our continued presence depended upon his questionable spirit of benevolence. An initial consignment, consisting of 3,000 zlotys, was divided into amounts of 1,000 for each of our two local patrons while Dr. Hladysz retained whatever remained. We learned through the latter recipient that Christine had recently set out on a journey to Radom and Warsaw, but as before, she encountered difficulties in both places. This effort indicated that Christine considered the task of helping me to survive a most vital one. But her business was not doing too well. And while transmitting funds directly from Munich she began to encounter obstacles. Even though, her initial transfer of 1,000 zlotys failed to reach me, Christine in a relayed message urged me to persevere.

Our eccentric host rendered aid in passing the many dreary hours by providing us with an accumulation of cloth and woolen remnants and from the latter we formed strings. Janina also fashioned useable jackets, socks, and gloves by unraveling discarded garments. We kept ourselves busy with such time-consuming tasks, but the limited daylight offered few benefits. Gradually our eyes adjusted to the lack of adequate illumination. Due to these occupational tasks we succeeded in retaining our emotional balance within this bleak environment.

Fortunately we continued to maintain a tenuous contact with the outside world and this enabled us to receive support from a small circle of friends. All postal remittances were sent to the address of Dr. Matinian and later on to Dr. Hladysz. Either recipient forwarded the money to Mr. Lachwicki. These funds enabled the latter, together with Mr. Bestetzky, to procure basic provisions even though much of it at times failed to reach us. Consequently, Dr. Matinian and Dr. Hladysz began to feel apprehensive and they knew that it would be best to send payments made out in our behalf through a different channel. Fortunately, an alternate approach presented itself. I proposed that Sophie, Janina's former maid in Cracow, should supervise all transactions from now on. This woman willingly complied with this request and the new channel for transmitting money soon began to function. Thanks to Christine's unfaltering effort our scheming benefactors appeared to be pacified, but their wish to exploit this source of money soon assumed greater dimensions. At times the registered letters contained 1,000 zloty banknotes, but every so often someone dared to remove them. Our benefactors could never find out who was responsible for these thefts.

When Christine was informed about this serious matter, she felt confused and dejected. She soon instructed her helpful associate to stop sending cash. It did not take long until our host became restless and wished to find out why the healthy milkcow ceased to provide him with benefits according to his expectations. He declared that things were supposed to be working out differently. We began to run short of provisions and dreaded the prospect of slowly starving to death. In order to prevent such a dreadful event from happening, Christine decided to send a registered letter directly to our host. To my misfortune this letter ended up in the hands of Mr. Wihan, the local postmaster. This man had a reputation of being a scoundrel who participated in the murder of Jews. Previously, while still inside the ghetto, he admired Christine's philatelically stamped envelopes. Finding them to be alluring, Mr. Wihan instructed one of his letter carriers to forward an invitation for me to pay him a visit. When I promptly showed up, he entreated me to give him the stamps for his collection. In return he offered to supply me with bread. Jews were absolutely forbidden to enter the post office premises, but for me he made an exception. So as not to be noticed I had to enter through the rear door. The postmaster, who liked what I gave him, told me that I was permitted to visit him anytime whenever I had interesting stamps.

This important letter was picked up by Mr. Wihan. He examined the envelope with care and then concluded that the Jewish philatelist was still alive and now he resolved to investigate the matter. Once again fortune, in the shape of Mr. Lazarewicz the assistant postmaster, smiled on me. This astute individual nurtured a most auspicious attitude. As soon as Mr. Wihan put the incriminating letter aside, Mr. Lazarewicz got hold of this piece of writing and had it delivered to our place of refuge. Surprisingly Mr. Wihan failed to question the disappearance of this letter and there ensued no confrontation. The following Sunday morning, while attending a church service, Mr. Lazarewicz told our host about what had taken place and advised him to be more careful in the future. As soon as the irritated host returned to his mansion, he told us about what transpired. I immediately composed a message to Christine whereby I cautioned her to desist from dealing with none but our reliable intermediary in Cracow. We dreaded the arrival of another incriminating letter and feelings of apprehension weighed heavily upon us for many days. We nurtured few doubts concerning Mr. Wihan's readiness to betray our presence to the German Security Service post in Zbaracz.

While the midsummer heat inundated this tormented land we persevered below its surface in a forlorn manner. The sun now shone brightly and the beauty of nature unfolded itself most splendidly while we, the fugitives, suffered continually from the dampness that permeated this cave. Brightness and natural beauty existed far above us while we languished in continual darkness.

On a vibrant violin
summer now sings his song.
Branches bend earthward,
Grass sinks down.

Roots and sprouts are thirsty,
Thirsty is my heart, as they are.
Often my heart enjoyed beauty,
But it never got enough.

If once I will descend,
to drink of Lethe, then above
over the vibrant violin
summer will play its song.

[Janina wrote a letter to Richard whereby she informed him about having survived a severe storm and her relocation to a different place. The boy was certainly able to recognize the meaning of this report which indicated that the ghetto had ceased to exist. While Richard was lodging with Sophie in her secluded apartment, the precarious position of the Jewish presence in Cracow worsened radically. In order to accelerate a ferreting out of Jewish hiding places, the Germans closed several main thoroughfares to vehicular traffic. Richard became alarmed when Sophie informed him about transpiring events. He was afraid that his counterfeit document would eventually become valueless. He assumed that the Germans would soon order him to drop his pants to see if he was circumcised. If such an event was destined to take place, they would surely arrest him on the spot. Overcome by anguish, Richard decided to leave Cracow at once. Sophie, who noticed the boy's state of apprehension, supplied him with nourishing durable provisions. She also gave him an adequate amount of money to pay for his return journey to Zbaracz.

Richard departed from Sophie's Lobszovska Street address at an early hour. He tried to avoid all main thoroughfares in order to evade a potentially disastrous encounter with German soldiers. He noticed with dismay that many of them were deployed at posts outside as well as inside the rail terminal. Richard feared that these armed men would most thoroughly inspect his travel permit while asking incriminating questions. An unpleasant encounter such as this seemed to be unavoidable. At the station, when asked, he explained that the purpose of his journey was to visit relatives. Richard's identity card was accepted as a valid one, and he received permission to board the waiting train.

Even though the coach was already filled with passengers, Richard managed to find a vacant seat. One hour after the train rolled out of the Cracow station it made an unscheduled stop near a small locality, located closer to Lvov, so that a group of armed SS soldiers could climb aboard. Soon they entered the car where Richard sat. One of the seemingly ill-disposed men who soon confronted the boy inquired: "What is the purpose of your journey to Zbaracz?" While struggling to stay calm, Richard replied instantly: "I am going to visit my sick aunt who lives there."

The Nazi inspector then asked to see his certificate. He closely examined the entry which identified the youngster as a Catholic, and then quickly concluded his inspection by returning the document to Richard. The meticulous SS man continued to carry out his duties, but to Richard's surprise he returned somewhat later in the company of another officer. The pair kept observing Richard from a nearby vantage post. They apparently waited for the youngster to become panicky and respond in a foolish manner. Richard, who felt quite uneasy, struggled to maintain his composure. This mounting sensation of anxiety caused his mouth to become dry while the two SS men did not relent in staring at the suspicious traveler. It seemed as if time threatened to stand still, but soon the intimidating examiners simply turned around and went away.

Having survived this close encounter, Richard felt emotionally drained. By now he anticipated harsh treatment upon being ejected from this railway car at the next stop where his circumcision would inevitably be uncovered. He dreaded the prospect of being exposed as a Jew and ending up in a labor camp or, worse yet, being quickly despatched from life to death by a bullet in the head.

When Richard finally alighted from the train in Zbaracz, he felt quite exhausted and besides he had no idea where his mother's sanctuary was located. He remembered that Dr. Hladysz maintained a cordial relationship with her, and he decided to go directly to the residence of this friendly woman. Richard had to knock several times on the housedoor until an elderly housekeeper opened it. Seeing a complete stranger standing there she became apprehensive. Richard wasted no time in introducing himself: "My name is Stefan Vlasovski from Krakow and I wish to see Dr. Hladysz. It is most important for me to do so."

Even though this startled housekeeper was confronted by a complete stranger, she allowed him to enter the doctor's place of residence. She could not fail to notice that this youngster suffered from exhaustion and quickly brought him a glass of tea. Dr. Hladysz, who soon entered the room, recognized Richard immediately but nearly fainted when she saw him. She knew that Janina's son had gone to Cracow but hardly expected him to return at this most critical time. Dr. Hladysz revealed to Richard that his mother had gone into a confidential hiding place in the home of Mr. Bestetzky. She also informed him about the horrific occurrences within this area and then instructed him in reaching the location of his mother.

Richard walked by himself to the house of Mr. Bestetzky without encountering difficulties. He repeatedly knocked on the front door and waited a long time until someone responded. When it was opened he looked with astonishment at a gaunt, somber-looking senile man. Mr. Bestetzky hardly anticipated meeting this youngster, and his unexpected appearance tended momentarily to confuse him. The owner of this estate told Richard to enter quickly but then declared that he could not accommodate him since he already had other guests. Richard readily identified himself as Janina's son and explained that he had no other place to go. The old man then went to fetch Janina, and after a tearful embrace she pleaded with folded hands to have mercy and permit the poor boy to stay with her. There ensued a drawn-out debate concerning the demanded payment for this additional tenant, but eventually Mr. Bestetzky emerged triumphant. Since Richard's clothes happened to be of reasonably good quality, our determined host insisted upon exchanging them for an old threadbare shirt and a well-worn pair of trousers.]

Richard, who now stayed with us inside this cold chamber, shared our unpleasant existence. Sophie had enough foresight to send a parcel which contained Richard's old clothes to supply him with additional and more suitable garments. Mr. Bestetzky also provided the youngster with a wooden board for him to sleep on. The three of us somehow whiled away the seemingly countless days within this well-hidden compartment. We were not allowed to benefit from the extending hours of sunshine and felt constantly chilled in this unhealthy environment. Being deprived of light and the beauty of nature we began to suffer from depression.

Besides, we dreaded the constant presence of the mentally disturbed woman who happened to be Mr. Bestetzky's wife. She lived in a world of her own and at times found it expedient to open the cellar door. She'd then shout: "You down there, be prepared to leave this house quickly!" Then again she'd exclaim: "The time has come for you to go home!" or: "From now on you people will have to cook for yourselves!" Various other dreaded emotional outbursts took place while we huddled below. Occasionally strangers, who had not been informed about our presence, visited this mansion but they always ignored her rantings. Once this mad woman brought us a bowl filled with chicken bones and upon inquiring what she wished us to do with them she replied: "I want you to turn them into glass!"

Mr. Bestetzky, who lived in a room on the upper floor, endured the dog days of summer but we suffered continually from the frigid air. Whenever the heat became unbearable he, dripping with perspiration, came down into the cellar to seek relief. Sometimes, when in a benign mood, he even brought us a newspaper. Janina, eager to receive news from the outside world, read the reports close by the opaque cellar window. Besides, being forced to endure the severe dampness, our noticeably deteriorating state of health caused me great mental anguish. I thought about what would happen if one of us became ill.

Once a sudden outbreak of a skin infection tormented us so much that we could hardly sleep. We logically assumed that living in this ominous location had caused our suffering. Since no physician could be summoned we greatly dreaded the thought of being overwhelmed by illness. By chance I came across a provocative ad in an old newspaper. It derived from a chemist's shop in Cracow which proclaimed the existence of a special tincture for eradicating skin infections. I decided to inform Sophie through our message-relay channel about this product. She responded quickly by sending me several small bottles filled with the wondrous substance. It took a while until the affected areas on our bodies showed an improvement. An additional hardship which afflicted us derived from our slowly disintegrating clothes. My shoes and shirt had already been partially reduced to tatters. Janina was more fortunate since Christine sent her several usable dresses.

We endured the passage of time with growing anxiety. Since the alloted space for moving about was most inadequate, our physical condition deteriorated steadily. Our solace derived mainly from reports about the rapid advance of Red Army forces. We now felt certain that our rescuers would soon be here, but it was impossible to know if we could stay alive until then. The weather slowly turned cooler with the approach of autumn, but this did not disturb us in our place of entombment.

One dreary day Dr. Matinian paid us a surprise visit. It seemed as if he wished to help us and we were glad to see him. This good doctor brought various pieces of cloth to work on as well as a blanket for Janina and Richard. He inquired if we received all of the money he entrusted to Mr. Lachwicki. This, however, was not done and it reenforced our suspicions concerning the landlord's lack of dependability. Even so, I implored Dr. Matinian not to mention the suspected embezzlement to anyone. We were, after all indebted to this eccentric man for allowing us to stay hidden inside his house.

Dr. Matinian climbed down into the cellar and with aroused curiosity he descended even deeper. Within this bleak atmosphere he began to feel shaken. While being confined in our gloomy and cold dungeon we always felt confused but thanks to Dr. Matinian some vital information about ongoing events reached us. For example, Mrs. Lina Weinsaft the dentist, who had succeeded in escaping from a moving freight train that carried Jews to their doom, found a place of concealment together with her elderly parents. Dr. Matinian claimed that only he knew where it was located. He strongly urged us to hold out until the approaching day of liberation.

[7]

The weeks of autumn brought us increasingly cool weather, but the steadily advancing Soviet armies were still a considerable distance away. The cold days with the many hours of darkness soon arrived here, and our tiny window was covered with frost while the damp straw bedding now served as a place of torment. What we needed to endure cannot easily be described. Surrounded by perpetual gloom and freezing temperatures, we suffered from extreme discomforts and dismay. Christine aided us continually with transmissions of money and provisions through her confidential assistants. Sophie, the maid, also sent us something by mail whenever possible from Krakow. These notable efforts enabled us to hold out literally from one day to the next. A message from Christine, postmarked January 5, 1944, arrived here during a dreary day and it was as follows: "I hope that you still have enough strength to carry on a few more weeks. Then we shall obtain whatever we need."

Another letter from Christine of January 17, 1944:

> Every day I ask myself whether there is any use in writing. Well, I will try, but have little hope. Every day I mull over the map and follow the events. I contemplate a lot, since there seems to be light, air, and sun again, and all the coldness will soon be over.

During the twilight hours of winter we remained active by sorting out discarded old clothes, supplied by Dr. Matinian and Dr. Hladysz. The avaricious Mr. Bestetzky showed up quite often to annoy us with requests for more money. The precarious contact with our benefactors was now interrupted and this worried us immensely. We feared that the greedy landlord might decide to reveal our presence to the authorities at the very last moment. The thought of being surrendered to the increasingly bad-tempered SS elite forces caused us to feel on edge. A threat of being subjected to unceasing extortion attempts transformed our precarious position into a desperate race against time. Christine was right when she declared that her efforts in our behalf, in spite of the many hazards, appeared as a necessary responsibility.

[One day Mr. Bestetzky told us that his irrational wife had recently spoken out of line while in the company of untrustworthy neighbors. She told them: "I cannot understand why these strange people are staying in our cellar!" The visitors, who were used to this woman's eccentric behavior, preferred to ignore her statements.

Once Mrs. Bestetzky nearly unleashed a panic while suffering from a seizure of agitation. She shouted loudly: "I warn you about the coming of the Antichrist. I am sure that he will soon be here and it would be best for you to leave us without delay!"]

In time my dental bridge began to show serious fractures which irritated my gums. The ensuing pain compelled me to conjure a method for removing it. Since the denture contained some gold I wished that someone who was able expertly to extract it would be present. Since I could not possibly visit a dentist, my only recourse was to perform the operation myself. Anticipating a painful ordeal, I embarked upon the task of detaching the denture from my gums. While proceeding with this stressful chore, I overtaxed myself. Even so my exertion proved to be successful. My jaw throbbed with pain and I spat out much blood, but the effort caused the tooth that served as an anchor for the denture to become detached. I managed to remove the tooth together with its bridge, but then I needed several hours to recover from my ordeal.

I gave this valuable object to our dumbfounded host who then brought it to Dr. Matinian. The good doctor paid him the sum of 3,500 zlotys. Mr. Bestetzky received nearly half that amount while Mr. Lachwicki had to be content with a smaller sum. The remainder of this money was not enough to obtain adequate provisions. Dr. Hladysz offered to provide us with simple tasks so as to pass the dreary hours in a productive manner. In return we received an additional supply of food.

Clearly motivated by the changing fortunes of war, the local baker began to deliver more bread. He also spoke about having seen long columns of battle-weary German soldiers as they retreated toward the west. They were obviously no longer able to impede the powerful thrust of a Red Army offensive which had already reached an area that was 100 kilometers away from Zbaracz. In response to this alarming situation, the local German military headquarters conscripted many able-bodied members of the local population to prepare defensive positions. They also instructed the Ukrainian militiamen to stand by to engage in battle. It happened that many of them failed to obey this call to action. Several days later a company of battle-fatigued

German infrantrymen, who were badly in need of a rest, demanded to be admitted into Mr. Bestetzky's mansion. These tired soldiers simply ignored the rantings of the landlord's wife while we stayed well hidden under a pile of straw. Several hours later the soldiers felt refreshed and decided to leave. Soon afterwards Mr. Bestetzky informed us about a German plan to evacuate this area. While supplying us with fresh bread and water he cautioned us to remain silent.

While hoping that our tenure of incarceration would soon come to an end, we felt as if a heavy burden was lifted from our backs. Many local residents were forced to assist in setting up obstacles even though the end of Nazi rule was in sight. Before a closing of the gate, so to speak, a most unpleasant event confronted us. Mr. Bestetzky came to inform us about unfolding events. He was now expected to provide quarters for a company of weary German soldiers. Later, he hinted that his house might have to be evacuated entirely. In response, we remained sitting as if on hot coals while time dragged on, but then our host eased the tension when he declared that this report was false.

When all postal services stopped functioning toward the end of February, a pervasive mood of desperation overwhelmed us since our provisions were nearly depleted. I knew that we could not possibly sustain ourselves until the arrival of Red Army troops. Our prolonged struggle for survival would have been in vain if their advance would somehow be delayed. A frightening event occured on Sunday, March 5, around five o'clock in the morning when a man shouted several commands in German and then pounded on the door. The host showed up later and informed us about the team of SS officers that made itself at home on the upper floor. He begged us to remain perfectly still and said that from now on we could not rely upon him for help. Even so, before abandoning us to our destiny he wisely provided a pailful of boiled potatoes. Mr. Bestetzky also installed a second bolt on the basement door which enabled us to lock it from the inside.

An unprecedented commotion reverberated throughout this aging structure while our ears became attuned to the tramping of heavy boots and the confusing babble of voices. More soldiers kept arriving in military vehicles while a radio communication center was being installed in Mr. Bestetzky's parlor. Other fighting men brought in campbeds to accommodate their officers. We shivered down below while expecting these men to invade our sanctuary and then overwhelm us instantly. Puffy, the housedog, annoyed by this hectic activity, barked furiously at the unfamiliar intruders. We, the helpless fugitives, experienced great difficulty in allaying our fear of being discovered. It was reasonable to assume that in the event of an air attack these German soldiers would most likely dash down into the cellar and upon discovery terminate our lives on the spot.

One of the landlord's neighbors, whose house had no cellar, had once made an attempt to enter our place, but Mr. Bestetzky strongly advised him not to do so. We, the suffering fugitives, had to remain out of sight no matter what happened. Plagued by unbearable feelings of tensions, we fervently prayed for an early arrival of the liberating armies. The next day, near sunset, the rumble of passing military vehicles abated even though loud roars from truck and tank Diesel engines remained audible. Whatever had wheels moved along at a rapid pace toward Tarnopol. This commotion reassured us that a German withdrawal was truly underway. Later, the rumbling from a diminished number of vehicles, involved in a headlong retreat, could still be heard.

Feeling completely overwhelmed by unsettling events, we prudently descended into the deep cellar. Approximately at eight o'clock in the evening a bright flare illuminated the surrounding landscape and soon there appeared a red one. These light signals were repeated several times and shortly thereafter powerful cannon explosions shook the ground. We realized that the outcome of this encounter would determine the nature of our immedite future. Janina and Richard, who seemed to be visibly shaken by the massive barrage, dressed quickly but I remained sitting atop a pile of straw as if in a coma. An overwhelming sensation of reassurance invigorated my soul. All I could say was: "I thank you ruler of the universe for ending our great suffering!"

I tried to console Janina who became very agitated by telling her: "Our journey is now drawing to a close. Have courage; God will help us survive!" Mr. Bestetzky soon called me from above, and I responded by opening the basement door. He let us know that the Red Army was expected to enter Zbaracz very soon. Even though he appeared to be in a very good mood the nerve-racking artillery continued throughout the night. Early next day, just after dawn, a company of Soviet soldiers appeared in our street. When that happened the elated Mr. Lachwicki came to inform us about the presence of many Russian soldiers in this town. They had already parked their armored vehicles and established a bivouac in the marketplace. This report convinced us that our longed-for hour of liberation had at last arrived.

Emotions of great rejoicing caused me to be almost speechless. Tears flowed freely as we thanked God for his benevolence. Our strange journey through the night had now come to an end as we nurtured hopes of soon emerging without hindrance into daylight. Soon a mood of anxiety replaced our feeling of gratitude. Our host, who wished to remain on good terms with his recently arrived armed guests, begged us not to reveal our presence for the time being. Two days later, some of these Russian lodgers happened to hear the sounds of human voices from below and quickly alerted their comrades to face unknown dangers. Several soldiers, resolved to find out the identity of fugitives, broke open the cellar door and then climbed down into our gloomy pit. When they found us sitting in this wretched tomb, one man asked: "Does this lair happen to be a clandestine base of operations?" While making feeble efforts to keep our limbs from trembling, we showed them what little remained of our documents. These hard-boiled combatants, visibly shaken by our appearance, expressed disbelief concerning our ability to survive in this dreadful environment.

Since our legs felt very stiff and appeared to be nearly useless, we did not have the strength to ascend the steps unaided. The soldiers helped us climb out of the cellar. As soon as I encountered the sun a great feeling of emotion surged through my brain and all I could say was: "Oh, the sun!" Indeed, the bright rays now illuminated a beautiful snow scene in all directions. Our sudden emergence into daylight, after having lived beneath the earth's surface for nine long months, was for us an extraordinary event. This took place four days after the Red Army reoccupied Zbaracz on March 9, 1944.

The sun, the lingering patches of snow, and the beckoning freedom threatened to overwhelm our senses. Since the pupils of my eyes adjusted slowly to the brilliance, I felt faint and unsteady on my weakened legs. Four weeks were needed to recover before I could walk normally. Initially, due to the brightness, our eyes were afflicted by intermittent pain and this forced us to shut them often. Our unsightly appearance motivated the Russian soldiers to treat us with compassion. Solicitous officers, as well as common soldiers, spoke words of kindness and even gave us small presents. They tried to console us by saying: "Now you are free and must not be afraid any longer!"

Some Red Army officers even invited us to share their meals, regardless of the fact that we wore nothing but worn-out and shabby clothes. Even so, they readily treated us as special guests of honor. Our liberators consumed nourishing food, but we ate sparingly in fear of abusing our perpetually near empty stomachs. The tears that welled up in my eyes were merely tears of joy.

[This occasion motivated an officer of higher rank to declare: "Now you have earned the right to select new clothes and shoes from an abandoned German army depot." In addition, we were given a chance to wash the accumulated grime with

soap and hot water from our abused bodies. This benevolent act caused me to feel
as if I had been reborn.]

My recollections of surreal acts of cruelty and the abysmal fear of an encounter
with pitiless SS butchers remains unforgettable. Whenever recurrent nightmares
about Nazi execution pits tormented me, I wailed in my sleep and then awoke trembling with fear. Whenever Janina noticed my nocturnal torments she roused and tried
to calm me.

> A bluebell flower, a pious one
> Rings in the evening,
> When I return from the day's sorrows,
> And it wants to comfort me in the evening.
>
> And I listen to its voice
> Clear as silver and tender as well,
> That the spark of my soul glimmer
> Into the peace of the evening.
>
> Because I am wood of a soft stem
> And the day cuts deeply into me
> And I believe, that the nurse
> Fed me when the bluebell called.

While armed encounters between opposing forces receded into the distance,
unprecedented events occurred daily. Even though a strict Soviet presence now dominated this land, an existence which resembled normalcy started to evolve. Even so,
Red Army soldiers and their officers continued to occupy Mr. Bestetzky's house.
These uninvited lodgers now passed the time by playing on instruments to the
accompaniment of lively tunes. Due to the steady coming and going of soldiers the
prevailing milieu kept changing from one day to the next.

It happened that a reporter, who worked as a representative of *Pravda*, the official Soviet newspaper, showed up. This journalist identified himself as Mr. Zeitlin
who was based in Moscow. He explained that he had been dispatched from that city
on a special assignment to interview survivors. Escorted by a representative of the
Soviet NKVD, he inspected our former underground habitation. After having done so
Mr. Zeitlin declared: "The survival of human beings under such extremely harsh circumstances is clearly beyond belief."

We gradually regained the use of our limbs and by April 17 felt strong enough
to go out and investigate what was left of Zbaracz. We saw a scaffold that stood at

the market square and upon it there hung the body of a police officer, still dressed in his uniform. Being unable to avoid an encounter with this sight, we recognized the corpse as having belonged to the SS Sturmführer Jetz. The Soviet rulers executed this notorious Nazi fanatic in retribution for the murder of at least 350 people. We stared for several minutes at the shabby remains of this killer and then quickly distanced ourselves from this dreadful site. Soon thereafter, overcome by exhaustion, we returned to our lodging.

We thought about what to do next, but for the time being we opted to remain in Mr. Bestetzky's old residence. There we came to occupy a bright and sunny room located on the upper floor. The green plants in this room were an invigorating change of scenery. For us, the first flowers of the spring season symbolized a renewal of life.

I realized that without Christine's determined efforts my life would have reached a bitter ending long ago. While exerting herself in my behalf, she seriously endangered her own existence. Even her mother used to express misgivings about my welfare. In my imagination I often assumed that she had taken the place of my own mother who died in 1926 while I was still a youngster in Budapest.

The days passed quickly as we progressed steadily on the way to recovery. When perpetually palefaced Janina developed a healthier tint, her steady improvement caused me to feel elated. The health of our host, on the other hand, declined noticeably. This Mr. Bestetzky impressed me as a most peculiar and frustrated individual. In spite of his willingness to shelter us during stressful times, he often appeared as an unpredictable and frightening apparition. He may have become afflicted by a malady which caused him to behave irrationally a long time ago. This misanthropic individual devoted much of his time to the maintenance of a magnificent garden where rows of black tulips and red roses thrived.

I soon felt a yearning to investigate the remains of our former ghetto area and embarked upon this dismal venture on June 25. Even though I anticipated my excursion to that place with great trepidation, I was determined to go there. Needless to say, this effort evoked considerable emotional pain. The pitiless Nazi despots compelled some 5,000 Jews to remain within a small area and now no more than a few empty huts remained. Most others had been reduced to piles of rubble. When I located my former abode only scant parts of that structure could be seen. Our synagogue building had also been reduced to rubble. I lingered for a short time amidst this devastation while trying to recall events of the recent past. Besides, I wanted to see the houses that had been severely damaged by recent armed encounters.

The local residents did not waste much time in making efforts to rebuild their old town while soldiers participated in removing the accumulated wreckage. I finally made up my mind to visit the site of our old graveyard, or more precisely where it used to be located. Parts of a stonewall still remained standing adjacent to the road. Within this hallowed precinct I beheld many damaged and uprooted gravestones amidst an expanse of tall weeds. The stately old trees that used to provide shade had been cut down many months ago and used for kindling while most gravestones were removed and utilized for the paving of streets.

A spirited atmosphere prevailed at the local market. Since all racially oriented directives had already been abolished, the Jewish inhabitants were now allowed to engage in commercial transactions. One heavy-hearted elderly Jewess sat silently among the vendors while displaying homemade cakes on a tray. She now took advantage of the new circumstance after having evaded several German entrapments.

One fellow survivor told me about a bizarre incident that involved a Christian woman who adopted a Jewish child before the final Aktion took place. When an SS executioner placed the little one on the ground next to the ravaged synagogue building, it, being unable to sense that death was near, remained silent. The killer aimed his pistol at the child's head and fired a shot but somehow the bullet missed its mark. The perplexed marksman refused to give up and once again he tried to kill the youngster. As if by miracle the little one remained unscathed. This singular event disturbed the cold-blooded assassin and recognizing this as a divine warning, he decided to spare its life. He then summoned a Ukrainian militiaman and told him: "Take this Jewish waif to your church to have it baptized." The orphan was admitted as a resident in the local municipal shelter upon having been turned into a Christian.

I made an effort to gather information concerning several other violent events. One of these dealt with the physical destruction of Mr. Gruenfeld together with members of his family at the hands of SS executioners. These zealous enforcers of Hitler's New Order wasted little time in despatching their victims from life to death.

Upon returning to Mr. Bestetzky's residence I tried to relax in his thriving rose garden while thinking about the violent deeds that were presently being investigated. During the nocturnal hours while sleep remained elusive I contemplated the distress of ill-fated ghetto inmates.

Several days later the Soviet military rulers decided to uncover the remains of all murdered Jews. This grisly task commenced at the main site on June 30, 1944. The execution trench contained the remains of those who were disposed of previously when the hideous fifth and sixth Aktionen took place.

Since German and Ukrainian executioners were held accountable for the murder of some 5,000 Jews within this district, the Soviet government decided to examine this event closely. The officially appointed body gathered evidence in relation to these genocidal activities. Local residents, military photographers, and Red Army officers, accompanied by sixty Jewish survivors, gathered next to this burial site at an early hour of the day. Janina, Richard, and I were present as well. Following the recitation of a short prayer the head of this delegation delivered a moving speech. Then, thirty able-bodied men, equipped with shovels, started to dig into the loose soil. Since the layer of earth was barely one-half meter thick, they uncovered several human remains within a very short timespan.

Among the first uncovered corpses was one that belonged to a young woman who still embraced a small child. This pitiful sight evoked loud cries of despair from the assembled spectators. Several of them appeared quickly to become emotionally drained from the chore of witnessing this stark scene. We felt most dejected when a group of photographers recorded this bizarre event, and soon we went away from this dreadful site.

The Soviet authorities then ordered investigations of several other gravesites to take place as well. Also, the remains of nineteen more people were uncovered in the vicinity of the legendary old castle. Among these I could still recognize the features of Mr. Oehl, his wife, and their little darling, Noemi. Besides, we were able to identify the body of our zealous physician, Dr. Kamelhaar, but his features were by now barely recognizable. Most victims, with the exception of small children, displayed gunshot wounds to the head, but the skull of one martyred person appeared to have been broken. We remained speechless while pausing at this gruesome site until the newspaper reporters finished taking pictures. The task of identifying the corpses required immense patience, and the powerful odor of decay caused all of us to feel nauseated.

These people who had been condemned to death had to dig their own graves. A local resident, who participated in the filling in of this ditch, reported that the crying of a child remained audible for a long time.

The Soviet inspectors uncovered another burial site on July 2. Located within the Lubianka forest, it contained the remains of seventy-two hostages whom the Germans arrested and then executed on September 6, 1942. Government officials expressed considerable interest in examining this site. Most uncovered human remains were still dressed in civilian clothes, and this enabled the investigators to retrieve documents from their pockets. Prior to being arrested, these people assumed that nothing worse than a performance of physical labor awaited them and hence they supplied themselves with sustenance for no more than a few hours. The murdered hostages found an eternal repose but we, the survivors who witnessed these genocidal proceedings, eagerly confirmed the validity of this monstrous crime.

Janina soon obtained some work, but for me there arose no opportunity to earn money. We became alarmed when the health of Mr. Bestetzky declined noticeably. It seemed to me that the life of this strange man would soon reach its end. I decided to summon a priest, who provided our sick landlord with a Christian absolution from sin. His soul then departed from its body on a sunny day in August. His unbalanced spouse, however, declined to recognize his demise. A strange young man, appearing out of nowhere, identified himself as the landlord's son. He walked directly to his father's room and while ignoring our presence began to seek out various useful items. His most valued acquisition consisted of a pocket-watch and a wallet that contained some money. Besides, he gathered little worn articles of clothing. This young Mr. Bestetzky remained unruffled throughout his short visit and then disappeared without saying a word. Not one solitary soul came to mourn the demise of our benefactor and no effort was made to remove his body. Finally, Janina assumed the task of notifying the local burial authority to carry our this urgent task. Puffy, the housedog who feared his master but liked us, failed to notice his absence as well. A most difficult man, whom God had selected as a tool for our salvation, was now gone from this world amidst such mysterious circumstances.

We received reports about devastating bombing raids over German cities while the trapped Nazi leader demanded ever more sacrifices from the hard-pressed remnants of his armed forces. Our contact with Christine was finally severed, and I could do nothing but hope that she would succeed in evading the disaster which now descended upon Germany. I prayed that with God's help she would succeed in surviving the impending catastrophe. In the meantime a fierce struggle between the two great powers continued, but current events clearly indicated that Hitler's Third Reich was destined to face its "Twilight of the Gods." I anticipated this day with great joy and looked forward to see Christine in the not too distant future.

We visited Mr. Studnitzky, the peasant in whose barn we stayed for one night. This man took all our posessions when we fled from the ghetto. The stolen goods remained in his posession, and when I brought up this matter, he replied: "I know nothing about it." Then he boasted about having donated our things to several Jewish causes.

The local Red Army commander declared that a celebration in honor of the Russian revolution would soon take place here. The gathering of Jewish survivors also planned to conduct a thanksgiving service. They wished to utilize the ruined synagogue for that purpose, but the participants consisted of a mere twenty souls. While standing at this hallowed site our spokesman eulogized the Jewish martyrs and enumerated their merits. He then recited an appropriate prayer for the well-being of their afflicted souls. It seemed as if the inexplicable Power of the universe wanted us to live on for a specific but still undisclosed purpose. I assumed that at this juncture of life we had a certain obligation to establish a testimony in reference to the deeds of our martyrs for the benefit of future generations.

While searching through the ruins of our former spiritual sanctuary, I came across the partly singed remnant of a Torah scroll. I wanted very much to keep this sacred relic and asked my fellow survivors for permission to do so. The lettered fragment would always remind me about the never to be forgotten encounter with callous evildoers.

I went through extremely stressful times while suffering from hunger and bitter cold temperatures. These prolonged traumas caused me to maintain an attitude of subservience in facing hostile Christians. Besides, I yearned to be back in Munich to resume my old life-style. I wondered if former friends who used to treat me in a gracious manner had survived the war.

Then came another November 9. The first in many years when we did not experience any anxiety. Without fear, without persecution, we still could not believe that our misery was finally over. Finally we could walk in the streets again with our heads raised. How many years did we have to walk around timidly and with our heads lowered? The memory of this is too much.

My health was not good due to my experiences. Also we had lost everything except our lives. Our appearance was more than pathetic; we were almost afraid to be seen in public. I had real homesickness for Munich!

Munich! What had become of this beautiful city and my beloved Munich citizens? I had spent a large and not the worst part of my life in this city of heart and merriment. Until 1933 nobody had ever heard a word of hostility here. When and where would I see Munich again? Would I find Christine under its rubble?

Finally the clock of fate moved on; the reports of German capitulation reached Zbaracz. Great festivities were the expression of our joy over this fortunate and long overdue turn of events.

Now there was no stopping. We were decided to take all hardships upon us just to get back to Krakow. We finally succeeded in traveling there in an open cattle car transport. In a somber mood we left Zbaracz and with it an important and decisive part of our lives.

Krakow was quite changed. There was nothing left of our former apartment. Sofie lived by herself in a modest place. She put us up readily and helped us to new clothing and to a relatively ordered way of life. But our goal was to see Christine. We had to reach Munich at all cost. Continuously, the savior of our life was the content of all our conversations. There was little chance that the two of us could obtain a travel permit in the foreseeable future. And to travel alone was impossible for me due to my poor state of health. I was intent on pursuing my plan to give Janina my name. Since fate had brought us together, and since we had experienced and overcome all our sufferings together, it was clear that God had destined Janina for me. Now the time had come to document this. Our ritual and civil wedding ceremony took place on June 26, 1945. We wanted to restrict our ceremony to a small circle, so only a few people participated in our simple and moving service. A loaded truck with Russian soldiers stood in the courtyard in front of the wedding office. There was a piano on one of these trucks and, just as we were getting married, we heard music from outside as if it had been ordered just for us.

Following the wedding ceremony we went to the cemetery where Janina wanted to visit the graves of her parents. But we found only stones, nothing else.

We encountered many difficulties obtaining the necessary travel documents. The Russian as well as the Polish armies were in charge. However, after much trouble we were able to obtain the papers. Then followed a difficult journey to Prague. There we were forced to obtain an additional document from the American office, which turned out to be quite helpful. This took another fourteen days. During this time our thoughts traveled ahead to Christine in Munich. It took us another week, however, before we could finally get the train there.

The encounter with this once so beautiful city was sad. Munich was hardly recognizable. Immediately we tried to find Christine.[5] We were both greatly relieved when we heard that she and her two sisters had remained alive, although her house had been destroyed three times in air attacks.

Finally we saw each other face to face again. We all had tears of joy in our eyes; Christine, our savior, was really in front of us again. Our goal to embrace and thank this noble person who had saved our lives was achieved. Without Christine we would certainly not be alive today!

May God reward Christine! We certainly cannot do this ourselves. With this wish my report shall end.

Postscript

The reader walked with me through the night. On this way he could observe my own personal fate which was certainly not singular in the great upheaval of the last years. There were many more things. But what is certainly not an everyday event and therefore even in our chaotic time worthy of publication is the very clear hand of God it shows. He alone led me securely through all the tribulations of death. God and nobody else. He uses people as his tool, who enter the stage of the drama at the right time, often at the very last minute, partly with selfish, partly with honorable reasons. He was able to improve clearly inescapable situations so the sun could break once again through the dark of the night.

Not only did individual people or entire nations walk on a doomed path through the night. The whole of mankind went on it. For a long time, before anybody saw it, the evening dusk descended on mankind and the spirit of the faithless and of materialism walked by its side. It is my hope that all of this will be behind us and that the renewed strength of the sun will shine once again over a world with its slowly healing wounds, whose scars shall be a warning sign for all of those who will follow us.

When I walked through Munich's streets still covered with ruins, I found almost everything which had once been dear to me destroyed. I recognized God's will in this symphony of destruction—to destroy all bridges to the past period of alienation from him and his will and to begin a new age from the rubble, the ruins, and the ashes.

My steps also led me to the place where my business had once stood, which I had built up with Christine in common labor and which had established my reputation in professional circles. I stood in front of nothing. This perception, this awareness of having lost everything left me completely untouched. I do not bemoan material things but those people who stayed behind on our common journey. They cannot be replaced.

Hatred, what a terrible word! Hatred caused everything. I do not believe that I had even one personal enemy in Munich except the above-mentioned hater R., with his purely material motives, and some of his followers. It gave them no rewards. God's unvarying justice finds its way to everybody.

Fear of God and trust in God were common in my family. I inherited them from my parents, who raised me with them and bequeathed them to me as their most valuable inheritance. My dreadful experiences only reinforced this belief in God in me.

A few weeks after my return a letter from my brother Miksa arrived from Budapest. He told me of the expulsion from Hungary of his two children and of his brother Lajos, who had all disappeared without a trace. This news agitated me immensely. Miksa himself had also been in a camp but with God's help had escaped alive. He continued in his letter: "I have only one wish left in my life, for which I pray to the Almighty with great intensity: To be reunited with you and my dear children, as well as with our brother Lajos."

My final reflections could not be finished in a better way than by a word which Miksa had written to me a long time ago:

> Let the envious be envious,
> Let the haters hate,
> What God gave to you
> They will have to leave to you!

Notes

1. November 9, was a holiday since the German Republic was proclaimed on that day in 1918. On November 7, 1938, a secretary in the German embassy in Paris, Ernst vom Rath, was assassinated by a 17-year-old Polish student named Herschel Grynszpan, whose parents had been deported to Poland earlier in the year with 15,000 other Polish Jews. On November 9, Hitler approved Goebbel's proposal for "spontaneous" demonstrations against Jews throughout Germany. The result was the infamous pogrom later referred to as *Kristallnacht* (Crystal Night), when synagogues and Jewish businesses all over Germany were set on fire and shattered glass littered the streets. Close to one thousand Jewish business were destroyed, about one hundred Jews were killed, and twenty-six thousand Jews sent to concentration camps. The Nazi government also imposed a collective fine of one billion Reichsmark upon the prostrate Jewish community. The hapless victims were thus made to sponsor the destruction of their own properties.

2. The *Sicherheitsdienst* (SD/Security Service) was dominated by a rigid organizational structure. The ghettos in Eastern Europe were administered by a branch of the *Geheime Staatspolizei* (GESTAPO), known as *Aussendienststelle* (External Service Department), which was divided into five sections. Section IV was in charge of matters pertaining to the treatment of Poles and partisans. Its main concern, however, dealt with the *Judenfrage* (Jewish Question). Similar to other sections in this evil structure, it was headed by an official with the rank of *Obersturmführer.* Its task consisted of directing exclusive military units called *Sonderkommandos*. Besides Germans and Austrians, these included Lithuanian and Ukrainian volunteers. Each unit, consisting of 45 to 150 men, was assigned the task of guarding ghetto perimeters, assisting in collecting candidates for liquidation, and taking part in their physical destruction. This procedure was referred to as *Sonderbehandlung* (Special Treatment). These callous murderers of civilians received provisions and payments from the Gestapo-Section IV.

3. The labor camp establishment in the eastern region included three basic categories. There existed regular labor camps, penal camps, and so-called Jewish

camps. The first division was attached to the *Deutsche Arbeitsfront* (German Labor Front). Recruitment centers supplied the human material, designated for maximum exploitation. Incoming candidates usually encountered primitive living conditions. Due to a low level of subsistence their ability to perform heavy labor remained minimal.

The second category consisted of *Straflager* (Penal Camps). These were subdivided into *Strafarbeitslager* (Punishment Labor Camps), *Zwangsarbeitslager* (Forced Labor Camps), and *Arbeitserziehungslager* (Work Education Camps). The objectives, pursued by all of these camps, remained identical. They consisted of exploiting the physical potential of each inmate to the fullest, even if it meant working him to death. The *Judenlager* (Camp for Jews), also known by its abbreviated form as JULAG, assumed an especially notorious character within the camp organization structure. An intense utilization of the Jewish labor potential produced extremely harsh living conditions similar to those that prevailed in concentration camps. These encampments began to function soon after Reichchancellor Hitler issued an order to proceed with his plan for mass murder. This unprecedented move envisioned the annihilation of the entire "Jewish race" wherever its members could be found. All those who were resilient enough to survive rigorous work schedules were eventually sent to a *Vernichtungslager* (Extermination Camp) for consignment to gas chambers and cremation ovens.

Forced labor camps were generally smaller than regular concentration camps and contained a population that varied from a mere dozen to several hundred. These establishments played an important role as places of confinement. Their staffs expended considerable efforts, in accordance with the wishes of the "ice-cold" Nazi leader, to accelerate the killing process. However, inmates that were classified as Aryans had a better chance of survival. Nevertheless, the death rate of those who had the misfortune of being confined inside these camps remained high. This was caused by unrelenting harsh treatment and constant overwork, accompanied by starvation diets. In addition, inmates succumbed to infectious diseases and catastrophic living conditions.

4. A bureaucrat, known as Hermann Mueller, was in charge at the Gestapo headquarter in Tarnopol, and there he supervised various nefarious proceedings. During the month of October 1942, SS soldiers gathered some one thousand Jews for a transport that was scheduled to convey them to the Belzec killing facility. Mueller planned to send another such shipment on November 8, 1942, and it consisted of a thousand additional Jews. An officer named Friedrich Katzmann was in charge of implementing the grandiose scheme known as *Endlösung der Judenfrage* (Final Solution of the Jewish Question) throughout the district of

Galicia. Having been empowered as an SS and security police leader in this area his prime task consisted of supervising the decimation of Galician Jewry. Soldiers that had been assigned to carry out this task reported increasing difficulties. This sinister scheme emanated from the main program, referred to as *Ausrottung des Judentums* (Extirpation of Jewry).

Katzmann, in one of his official dispatches, reported the following: "There are many Jews who succeed in running away and they try to find hideouts in locations such as sewers and chimneys. While hiding inside cellars, attics, excavations, and bunkers they seek to evade our patrols. As the Jewish population decreases in numbers its determination to resist increases. They are now starting to oppose our efforts with diverse types of weapons, including those of Italian origin. It is evident that these arms derive from Italian soldiers who are stationed in this area. We also uncovered underground bunkers with superbly camouflaged entrances. In most instances these permitted no more than one person to enter at a time. All approaches to these strongholds are well hidden so that it was difficult for us to locate them while being unfamiliar with the surrounding terrain. We had to rely on Jewish captives whom we promised anything in order to obtain their cooperation."

The German military authority issued the following report: "Three large bunkers had been constructed by Jewish activists in the ghetto of Rohatyn. One of these, located at an elevated spot, is thirty meters long. There we uncovered a waterspout and a toilet. We also found an installation for generating electric power together with a radio receiver. The antenna of this device was hidden inside the chimney of an adjacent building. It also provided a means of ventilating the bunker during daylight hours and as a smoke exhaust for a kitchen stove used only during the hours of darkness. The bunker contained several two and three-level bunk beds that were supplied with linen. Tables and benches, together with cooking utensils, were also available for the occupants of this place. We uncovered an adequate supply of food to maintain sixty persons for an extended period of time. Some other bunkers, exposed by means of disclosure, existed there as well.

"During the time of this *Aussiedlungsaktion* [Resettlement Action] we uncovered the attempted flights of several Jews. The ones who embarked upon a venture to get out of this country had money, jewelry, and forged documents in their possession. These people dared to approach German, as well as Italian and Hungarian military truck drivers and offered to pay them up to 5,000 zlotys for being taken to a frontier. Some of these soldiers, especially Hungarians and Italians, readily agreed to accommodate the Jewish fugitives. Many of these escapees were recaptured by undercover agents of our security police. This effort then enabled us to confiscate their assets.

"Since increasing reports concerning Jewish resistance attempts reached us we were compelled to apply forceful means in eradicating these bandit activities. Accordingly, our SS formations proceeded to liquidate the Jewish ghetto in Lemberg during June 1943. So as to minimize our losses in manpower we concentrated our offensive action in places where we suspected the presence of bunkers. After having set a number of buildings on fire we flushed out an astonishing total of 20,000 Jews. While our cleansing operation was in progress we came upon some 2,000 corpses in various secret locations. A large number of fugitives, who opted to terminate their own lives, had swallowed poisonous substances. Losses sustained by our forces during this operation were as follows: Victims of spotted fever—18 men dead and 120 men sick. Victims of Jewish assaults—7 men dead and 12 men wounded. Victims of accidents that occurred during the time of Jewish resettlement—2 men dead and 5 men wounded.

"All SS troops and police units made great efforts and their spirits remained high from the beginning until the end of this operation. By devoting themselves to assigned duties, they performed well during the time of insertion into this engagement. Due to a great devotion to duty alone was it possible for our soldiers to eradicate this spreading pestilence in the shortest possible time."

5. Several years after Jakob Littner's death, one of his daughters, now known as Yolan Grey, decided to establish contact with Christine Hintermayer in Munich. In a letter addressed to her, Mrs. Grey requested information about her father's old suitcases, allegedly filled with a large number of rare postage stamps. Christine, in her reply, explained that the stamps in question had already been evaluated by a local philatelic auction house at a considerably lower price than expected. Besides, the suitcases formerly owned by Jakob Littner had mysteriously disappeared some time ago. Later, in 1968, Mrs. Grey embarked upon a trip to Europe. While staying in Munich, she visited one of her father's former acquaintances who also bought and sold postage stamps. While discussing topics of common interest, this man declared: "Since you are here in Munich, it would most likely interest you to take a look at Christine's thriving business establishment at the Stachus." This stimulated Yolan's curiosity, and the following day she walked over to the given location. While standing at the busy thoroughfare near this well-known dealership, her desire to meet Christine face to face dissipated rapidly. Far too many disturbing events had taken place in this great city, and suddenly she lost her desire to recall past traumatic events. Yolan promptly walked away from Christine's grand enterprise and wished never to see this place again.

A Review of Events that Took Place in the Region of Zbaracz, Lvov, and Tarnapol

During the years of Nazi German occupation the Jewish residential districts were segregated from all Christian habitations. The inhabitants of the Jewish districts were forced to endure a systematic process of decimation. This was accomplished by means of repeated assemblies, referred to as *Aktions*. These dreaded efforts were carried out by specially indoctrinated military units of the Nazi party, known as *Schutzstaffel* (Protective Squad), supported by Ukrainian assistants. These sadistic tormentors of helpless people dealt with their victims in a brutal manner. An administrative body which functioned as a tool for the carrying out of vicious German demands, known as *Judenrat* (Council of Jews), was also created during that time. A Jewish quasi-military unit, known as *Ordnungsdienst* (Enforcement Service), supported this demeaning directorate. Its prime task consisted of aiding the German *Einsatztruppen* (Insertion Troops) in the gathering of Jewish candidates for physical liquidation.

Soon after German forces went into the area of Zbaracz, Lvov, and Tarnapol, they gathered the entire local Jewish population in Zbaracz. A company of SS soldiers arrived there on September 16, 1941, to arrest all Jewish intellectuals and community leaders. They escorted them into the nearby Lubienicki (Littner: Lubianka) forest in order to terminate their lives. The Gestapo leader in charge of the district of Tarnopol was known as Hermann Mueller and his assigned task consisted of supervising the destruction of Jews within this area. Nearly 600 infirm and elderly captives were killed outright during the spring of 1942 while the healthier and younger ones were sent to the Kamenka-Bugskaya and Zborow labor camps. The German overlords transferred some thousand Jews to the death camp of Belzec and to the Lvov-Janovska labor camp between October 20 and October 22, 1942. A transport, consisting of some thousand Jews was assembled and dispatched to Belzec during November 8 and 9, 1942. An SS *Sonderkommando* troop came to execute several hundred Jews in a specially prepared trench on April 7, 1943. The decimated ghetto ceased to exist soon afterwards on June 8, 1943. When Red Army troops arrived to liberate Zbaracz, they found sixty Jews who were still alive.

The Jewish presence within the area of Tarnopol, according to annals, dates back to 1510. Some 18,000 Jews lived there in 1939. Nearly 5,000 of them were put to death between July 4 and July 11, 1941 upon the arrival of German forces. Then the Gestapo chieftains invited 63 Jewish intellectuals to attend a meeting at their head-quarters. As soon as these men showed up they were killed. The German invaders drove some thousand Jews into the nearby forest where they executed them on March 25, 1942. While this went on large numbers of Jews were seized in the streets and taken to forced labor camps. Nearly four thousand of them were arrested on September 30, 1942, and sent to the Belzec killing facility according to the wishes of the paranoid German leader. The pitiless Nazi tyrants brought all surviving able-bodied Jewish men to a nearby labor camp during the following winter. The Tarnopol ghetto ceased to exist on June 20, 1943, and the labor camp on August 6, 1943. When Soviet forces recaptured Tarnopol, some 150 Jews emerged from various hideaways while 200 more returned from the Soviet Union's interior.

The Jewish presence in the larger city of Lvov (Lemberg) dates back to 1340. It consisted of approximately 150,000 souls during the summer of 1941. This however included several thousand refugees from Western Poland. There the Ukrainian Christian population was encouraged to attack the defenseless Jewish community. During three days of unrestrained violence, thousands of Jews faced imprisonment and torture but most of them were eventually murdered. Several thousand prominent Jewish denizens were seized during the month of July and killed through the course of a cruel event, named *Aktion Petlyura.* It lasted from July 25 to July 27, and ended in the slaughter of more than two thousand Jews. Simultaneously, a labor camp became operational near Lvov. This dreadful installation caused many of its inmates to lose their lives due to physical abuse and extremely harsh living conditions. Others were murdered as soon as they entered this facility.

The Jews who faced confinement within a small perimeter in Zbaracz endured severe torments due to malnutrition and infectuous diseases during the winter of 1941 to 1942. Ruthless SS troopers conveyed some 15,000 Jews to an extermination facility during March 1942. An extensive Aktion that lasted from August 10 to August 23 within this region claimed the lives of nearly 40,000 ensnared Jews. At the conclusion of this hideous event, SS Gruppenführer Fritz Katzmann ordered the securing of a quaranteened area wherein several thousand detainees succumbed to the ravages of epidemics. Nearly 15,000 Jews also lost their lives while being detained at the Belzec and Janovska camps.

The final Aktion took place during July 1943. At that occasion the remaining 20,000 Jews opted to offer armed resistance, but inevitably most of them perished. Some 7,000 survivors, who ended up in the Janovska camp, were then slaughtered. The district of Lvov-Lemberg was declared as having been rendered *Judenrein* (cleansed of Jews) even though some fortunate ones succeeded in finding sanctuaries among compassionate Christians.

Nearly three million people, comprising ninety percent of the Polish-Jewish community failed to survive the terrible years of German occupation. No more than 60,000 Jews outlived the senseless slaughter. One association, consisting of some 180,000 people treked back from the Soviet Union's interior. The Ukrainian Jewish population numbered approximately 1,500,000 souls, but sixty percent of them failed to survive the war. Many Jews who returned to their former homes in Poland encountered intense feelings of animosity and severe violence. Holocaust survivors found safe harbors inside displaced persons' camps that opened up throughout Western Europe. Most of these homeless people wished to leave these emergency shelters as soon as possible by emigrating to Palestine. Some 250,000 Jews resided in these places of temporary refuge since they offered an opportunity to obtain certain types of vocational training. After an independent state of Israel came into existence on May 14, 1948, many displaced Jews went there to become useful citizens while others received special visas for settling in the United States of America. Those who opted to remain in Poland and the Ukraine were indeed few in numbers.

Jakob's Littner's graduation certificate from the Hungarian-Israelite Agricultural and Industrial Trade Association, Budapest, May 13, 1900.

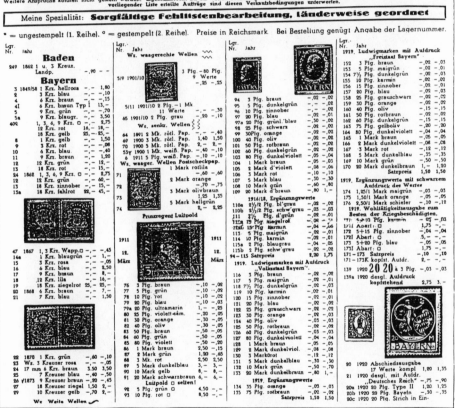

Philatelic price list from Jakob Littner's stamp dealership in Munich.

Jakob and Katherine Littner's children, Zoltan, Lilly (Yolan), and Hedda.

Nazi handbill: "ARYANS BUY ONLY FROM ARYANS."

The last *Passierschein* (permit) issued by Mr. Schmajuk, chairman of the Judenrat in Zbaracz, on June 8, 1943. It reads: "The Jew Littner is authorized to leave the Jewish residential quarter. Purpose: Medical assistance. Valid from June 7, 1943, to June 8, 1943. The chairman of the Jewish Council (Schmajuk). Littner: "We left the Ghetto at 2 p.m. The final cleansing operation (*Saübersaktion)* in the ghetto commenced during the same night. In the morning all of the remaining inhabitants were dead."

Jacket art of the 1948 edition of Jakob Littner's *Aufzeichnungen aus einem Erdloch*. According to Eckhard Haack, editor of the 1985 facsimile edition of the book, the artist was Hans Grundig. Born in Dresden in 1901, he was a founding member of ASSO (Association revolutionärer bildender Künstler Deutschlands) and was included in the Nazi exhibit "Entartete Kunst" (Decadent Art). Arrested in 1936, rearrested in 1938, he spent 1938–44 in Sachsenhausen concentration camp. In 1946 he became the first director of the Dresden Hochschule für Bildende Künste and died in 1958.

A view of the Zbaracz ghetto area located next to the horse market. April 1943. This drawing and the two that follow appear in the typescript of Jakob Littner's "Mein Weg durch die Nacht," but they do not appear in Littner's *Aufzeichnungen aus einem Erdloch*. It is not known whether they were drawn by Littner or someone else. This drawing of the Zbaracz ghetto bears a strong resemblance to the art on the jacket of *Aufzeichnungen,* although clearly done by a different artist.

Interior view of hut in ghetto. The bunker is shown beneath the table.

The hiding place in the deep cellar from June 8, 1943, until March 9, 1944.

Zoltan Littner. He and his wife died in the Warsaw ghetto in 1943.

Mietek Korngold. He was murdered on April 7, 1943, in Zbaracz.

"Our life-saver Christine Hintermaier."

Remains of a Torah scroll found by Jakob Littner in the ruined synagogue of Zbaracz.

Exumation of shooting victims by Red Army soldiers at the execution site.

The reburial of execution victims. Present are Red Army soldiers and survivors, including Janina and Jakob Littner.

Membership Cert. No. 105
Mitglieds-Karte Nr.

Bearer of this Mr., Mrs., Miss
Inhaber dieser Karte Herr, Frau, Frl.

L i t t n e r Jakob

date of birth   Place of birth
geb. 17.4.83   zu Budapest

is member of Israelitischen Kultusgemeinde
in Munich
ist Mitglied der Israelitischen Kultusgemeinde in München

Munich,
München, den 8. Oktober 194 5

(Community of Israelitic Worship
and Instruction)
Israelitische Kultusgemeinde
München, Herzog Maxstr. 7

Signature of bearer
Eigenhändige Unterschrift des Inhabers

Name and Christian name
(Vor- und Zuname)

At withdrawal this certificate
will be given back to the Kultusgemeinde
Dieser Ausweis ist beim Ausscheiden
aus der Kultusgemeinde zurückzugeben

Jakob and Janina Littner with his brother Miksa Littner from Budapest in Munich, 1946.

Janina and Jakob Littner in Munich, 1945.

Janina and Jakob Littner in New York, December 1947.

Headstone in Beth David Cemetery in Elmhurst, New York.

Kurt Nathan Grübler

Other Books of Interest from Continuum International

A Jump for Life
A Survivor's Journal from Nazi-Occupied Poland
Ruth Altbeker Cyprys
With a Foreword by Martin Gilbert

"A spellbinding Holocaust memoir by a woman who lived in the Warsaw ghetto from the beginning to almost the end in 1943.... This amazing story of courage, cruelty, and compassion will keep young adults turning the pages to the end."
— *School Library Journal*

"Well written and edited, the journal reads like a thriller.... A gripping account of a Jewish woman's determination and resolve to survive the Holocaust; highly recommended."
— *Library Journal*

The History of an Obsession
German Judeophobia and the Holocaust
Klaus P. Fischer

"Fischer writes with a clear mastery of both primary and secondary sources, synthesizing a wide spectrum of literature into a fine, scholarly work. Highly Recommended."
— *Library Journal*

"This is a truly significant work, for Fischer gives a balanced account of a complex subject, making it painfully clear just how Germany became capable of genocide."
— *Booklist*

"A detailed, well-written, sober and analytic study that deserves the widest possible circulation.... Although the rise of Nazism has been told many times, Fischer makes a clearly reasoned, well researched attempt to put a horrible crime and a horrid epoch into an appropriately complex historical context."
— *Publishers Weekly*

The Holocaust and the Christian World
Reflections on the Past, Challenges for the Future
Edited by Carol Rittner, Stephen D. Smith, and Irena Steinfeldt

"The editors have gathered together a multi-faceted collection of reflections on one of the most painful subjects to come out of the Holocaust. Eschewing oversimplification, the editors offer the findings of some of the most important authorities in the field. Highly recommended as an absolutely reliable introduction to a singularly complex yet important subject."

> —Richard L. Rubenstein
> Director of the Center for the Study
> of Religion, Ethics and International Affairs
> University of Bridgeport, Connecticut

"This book meets a long standing need....[It] provides a balanced yet razor-sharp perspective on the events that have drawn diverse interpretations and evaluations....A welcome contribution not only to the history of this terrible time, but to the possible futures that may still emerge."

> —Margaret A. Farley
> Gilbert L. Stark Professor Christian Ethics
> Yale University Divinity School

"How was it possible? The Nazi genocide of the Jews—the people of Jesus himself, the Virgin Mary and the first Christians—took place in the heartland of Christian civilization. To make sure that nothing like it ever happens again is our plainest duty. Prepare to be challenged and moved."

> —Clifford Longley
> *The London Tablet*

Understanding the Holocaust
An Introduction
Dan Cohn-Sherbok

Designed as a text for students in colleges and universities as well as for the general reader, this study contains both history of the Holocaust and extensive reflections on the ethical, cultural, and religious issues to which it gives rise.

※　　※　　※

Ethics after the Holocaust
Perspectives, Critiques, and Responses
Edited by John K. Roth

The book's six contributors — experienced Holocaust scholars from the fields of literature, philosophy, religious studies, and theology — attempt to answer the question: Where were the ethical traditions and teachings that seemingly should have kept such a catastrophe from occurring? The book's distinctive dialogue format deepens inquiry that interprets the Holocaust not only as an assault on millions of innocent human beings but also as an attack on goodness itself.

※　　※　　※

Teaching the Holocaust
Ian Davies

Incorporating substantial introductory material, a variety of perspectives, and practical case studies, an international team of contributors offers pragmatic strategies for teaching this complex topic while stressing the importance of passing down lessons of the Holocaust to future generations. This book will appeal to those involved in teaching history, humanities, and social studies at the high-school level.